KARṆA

Villain or Victim? A Journey Through Dharmic Shadows

AKSHAT DUBEY

I wanted to dedicate this book to Gitapress , my revered Gurudev ,Shankaracharya of Puri matt and my friend Mayur Pandey. From Gitapress and Gurudev I recieved the knowledge and inspiration that formed the foundation of this work. Their teachings and guidance illuminated the path I followed throughout this journey. I am especially grateful to my friend Mayur Pandey, whose unwavering support and valuable suggestions greatly helped and motivated me in designing and shaping this book.

CONTENT

PREFACE

Karna is often painted as the tragic hero of the Mahabharata—an unfortunate victim of fate, wronged by society, and denied the honor he supposedly deserved. For centuries, he has been glorified as the epitome of loyalty, generosity, and valor. But is this image of Karna entirely accurate? Or is it a carefully constructed myth, shielding his darker shades from scrutiny?

This book seeks to unravel the truth behind Karna, peeling away the layers of romanticized victimhood to examine his actions through the lens of Dharma and Adharma. Was he truly an unjustly persecuted hero, or was he a man whose ego, unchecked ambition, and questionable choices led him to his downfall? Did he uphold righteousness, or did he compromise his morality for his allegiance to Duryodhana?

By diving deep into his words, deeds, and allegiances, this book will explore whether Karna was a misunderstood warrior or a man who knowingly walked the path of Adharma, justifying his flaws under the guise of misfortune. The Mahabharata is not just a tale of black and white; it is a story of choices, consequences, and moral dilemmas. And Karna's journey, often shrouded in sympathy, deserves to be seen in its entirety—without selective amnesia or emotional bias.

Prepare to embark on a journey through the Dharmic shadows, where we confront Karna—not as a glorified martyr, but as a man whose legacy may not be as righteous as many believe.

AKSHAT DUBEY
Maghi Purnima, Shukla Paksha
Vikrami Samvat 2081

ACKNOWLEDGEMENTS

I extend my deepest gratitude to readers for your invaluable contribution to this book. Your keen eye for detail, thoughtful editing, and creative vision in designing the cover have truly brought this project to life. Your dedication, patience, and expertise have made this book better in every way.

Thank you for your unwavering support and for being an integral part of this journey. I am incredibly grateful for your hard work and the passion you poured into every aspect of this book.

With appreciation.

1. BIRTH

Once upon a time, in ancient times, an aggressive and ferocious saint named "Durvasa" came to King Kuntibhoj. The great ascetic said to the king Kuntibhoja, "O King who is free from envy! I wish to eat alms in your house, but on one condition: neither you nor your servants should act against my wishes. Only if you accept this condition shall I reside in your house". Then King Kuntibhog gladly accepted the saint's request and appointed his daughter "pritha", also known as kunti, to serve the great saint. Princess Kunti, observing a strict fast and maintaining a pure heart, began to serve the great Brahmin diligently. Often,he would leave,saying, "I will return in the morning".Yet Kunti never shoed any irritation.Instead,she offered him more and more food each day,alone with increased comfort such as bedding.Nothing was lacking in her service. Sometimes the sage cursed them or uttered harsh words.At times,he did'nt come for days and,upon returning suddenly,demanded food but Kunti always served him food wholeheartedly. After a year of rigorous service, the great sage Durvasa was pleased and said "-bhadre! I am delighted by your devotion. Ask me for boon one that is rare and capable of surpassing beauty of all women. Then she gently replied, "O Great brahmin, your blessing upon me and my father are more then enough. I don't desire any boon". Even though she refused the sage pleased by her humility,gave her a mantra.it had power to summon any deva and obtain a child from them . After giving her this gift,returned to his ashram.One day,while lying on her bed, her eyes fell upon the sun.Out of curiosity, she recited the mantra given to her.Suddenly, she was granted the divine vision. The rays of the sun did'nt hurt her eyes. Then appeared Bhagwan Surya, adorned with divine armour and earrings. He said "O dear one! I have come under your control-drawn by the power of mantra.tell me, what shall I do for you" listening this Kunti politely refused to take anything from him.Hearing this, Bhagwan Surya dev said,"O, Kunti! It is unjust to summon a Devtaand then dismiss him.I know you desires a son.So I shall grant you a child who will be born with divine armour and earrings ". Listening this Kunti become anxious, fearing her family honor and purity. She said "what will society think?what will my family and future husband say? This will ruin my honor".Suryadev consoled her, promising that she would remain pure and that the child would be born with divine qualities.He assured her that her virginity would be remain intact. By his yogic power, Surya established his effulgent energy within her womb while preserving her purity.

 just like the moon rises in the sky in the same way, on the Prathipada of the shukla paksha in the eleventh month, Kunti conceived the child of Surya.
 Kunti Devi concealed her pregnancy from her family,

sharing it only with her nurse. She stayed in the inner chamber of the palace to keep it hidden.When the time came, by the grace of Surya, she gave birth to a radiant child.He had divine armour on his chest and golden earnings like surya dev himself . The boy was wearing a shield on his body like his father, Suryadev. The child had eyes like a lion and shoulders like a bull.After the child was born, KuntI consulted her nurse.They placed the baby in a soft, beautifully prepared box, sealed it with wax to prevent water from entering, and closed it with a lovely lid. With a heavy heart, Kunti placed the box into the river and returned home in tears—crying for the son she was compelled to abandon.

The floating box was found by Adhirath, a charioteer and close friend of King Dhritarashtra. Along with his wife Radha, he adopted the child and raised him as their own. That child would later be known as Karna.

2. CHILDHOOD

MISCONCEPTION

In the previous chapter, we explored Karṇa's birth and how he was born to Kunti and SuryaDev. The main misconception about Karṇa's life begins from his childhood.Various writers & scholars like Ram dhari singh dinkar, Ranjit Desai due to their communist mindset and desires to promote a mythical hero for their agenda,portray him as poor boy from a lower caste background.But in reality, he was adopted by a wealthy family of high status. His father, Adirath, was a charioteer and a close friend of King Drithrasthra. As mentioned in the 309th chapter of the kundalharan parva (Vanparva)

एतस्मिन्नेव काले तु धृतराष्ट्रस्य वै सखा। सूतोऽधिरथ इत्येव सदारो जाह्नवीं ययौ

At this very time, however, he was a friend of Dhritarashtra. The charioteer and his wife went to Jahnavi as Adhiratha.

From this, it becomes clear that Karṇa did not belong to a poor family but to a prosperous and influential household . Another widespread misunderstandings is about his caste "suta". It is often falsely claimed that sutas were of a low caste, However, according to the 16th chapter of kichakvadha parva (Viratparva)

ब्राह्मण्यां क्षत्रियाज्जातः सूतो भवति पार्थिव। प्रातिलोम्येन जातानां स होको द्विज एव तु

Rajan! A child born to a Kshatriya father and a Brahmin mother is called 'Sutta' among varn shankar only this thread caste is called Dwija.

Thus, Karṇa had a status equal to a Kshatryas though not a prince. Soon, he becomes an integral part of the Kuru family. Just like his father, he also becomes close to Duryodhan. When the Pandav arrived in Hastiunapur, Karna's bond with Duryodhan grew stronger. In competition like archery, wrestling, and racing, Kauravs and Karn always tries to rebuked Pandavas but failed to match their skills. Seeing this, Duryodhan, Shakhuni, and Karṇa plotted to kill Bhimsen, who was the bone marrow of the pandas, by feeding him Kalkut poison.However, the plan failed miserably and only served to increase Bhimsen's strength. King Drithrasthra then began searching for a guru for princes.At that time Dronacharaya happened to enter Hastinapur. Therefore, after a demonstration of his skills to young princes,they were impressed and conveyed the news to Bhishma pitamaha. After discussing with Vidur and King Drishrathra, Bhishma appointed Dronacharya as the Guru of the princes, rewarding him with wealth and royal hospitality. Dronacharya pleased with the gesture accepted both Kauravs and Pandavas as his disciples and begine their training. One day, in private, Dronacharya asked his students, "I have a deep desire in my heart, and after you complete your training, you have to fulfill my wish". Listening to this, all the princes remained silent. Only Arjun came forward and took an oath to fulfil his guru's wish. Then the Acharya embraced Arjun and blessed him. From then on, Dronacharya trained the princes with great intensity.Soon,many princes from different kingdom including Vrishni, Andhaka and even sutaputra Karṇa, came to him to learn under him, as mentioned in Sambhava parva (Adiparva)and Kundalharan Parv (vanparva).

सूतपुत्रश्च राधेयो गुरुं द्रोणमियात् तदा ॥ ११

And Radhanand Karṇa came to Dronacharya to learn the art of archery.

तत्रोपसदनं चक्रे द्रोणस्येष्वस्त्रकर्मणि
सख्यं दुर्योधनेनैवमगमत् स च वीर्यवान्

There, he accepted the discipleship of Acharya Drona to learn Dhanurveda. In this way, the valiant Karṇa became friends with Duryodhan;

This shows Dronacharya never discriminated against Karṇa for his caste,as falsely portrayed by many communist scholars and TV shows which spread hatred and dishonesty against brahmins.

Karṇa had great envy towards Arjun from childhood due to Arjun brilliance in archery. This jealousy deepened Karṇa's alliance with duryodhan, and the two become more than friends "brother".Together they regularly insulted Pandavas and conspired against them as mentioned in Kundalharan Parva (Vanparva).

संधाय धार्तराष्ट्रेण पार्थानां विप्रिये रतः
योद्धमाशंसते नित्यं फाल्गुनेन महात्मना ॥३१॥

Having joined hands with Duryodhana, son of Dhritarashtra, Karṇa was engaged in causing harm to the sons of Kunti and was always expressing his desire to fight with the great-hearted Arjun.

Thus, it is incorrect to believe Karṇa had a miserable childhood, just as scholars and TV shows portrays.He grew up with wealth , prestige and friendship with royalty. He envied Arjun not because of his privilege but due to his mastery in archery . Later Karṇa aproached Bhagwan Parshuram for higher learning.Many Scholars wrongly claim that Dronacharya refused to teach him for caste.But in reality, Dronacharya taught him every thing except Brahmastra, as he sensed envy, hatred and arrongance in Karna's heart.Seekinng knowledge of Brahmastra, Karna lied to Parshuram about his varna. As a result,Parshuram cursed him.This was just punishment,our scriptures states that one must not never deceive their Guru or Parents for,they are the ones who gives us new life and shape our journe

TOURNAMENT OF PRINCES

After the completion of the princes'training, Guru Dronacharya decided to organize a tournament where princes could showcase their skills of weapons before the public and demonstrate the power of Hastinapur royal lineage.He presented his proposal to King Drithrasthra, saying, "O King! Your sons have completed their training in the art of weapons. If you permit, they should demonstrate their art of handling weapons." King Drithrasthra happily agreed,and preparation for the tournament begins.On the decided day, King Drithrasthra, along with minister, Bhishma ,Acharya Drona and Kripacharya arrived at the arena, which was magnificently decorated with pearls, gold studded walls and flags. People of all the varnas rushed from the city,eager to witness skill of the princes. In no time large crowd gathered there and arena got filled . After the sacred rituals were completed , the valiant princes of the Bharat dynasty, entered the arena.Dressed in an armour, equipped with bows, and mounted on their chariots, they saluted to Acharya Drona,and Kripacharya before taking their positions. At Dronacharya's command, the kauravs were the 1st to take up their arms.Adorned with gold arnaments, they performed various feats- climbing ropes , aiming arrows and striking target. They demonstrated horse back riding , sword fighting, elephant warfare, and other combat techniques. The audience was mesmerizedby their grace, speed , strenght and , mastery over weapons .

Then came the most anticipated event,the mace duel between Duryodhan and Bhimsen, who were known for their fierce rivalry . They entered the battlefiled with maces in hand ,looking like two towering mountains . The battle between the two princes begans, and it becomes so fierce that Guru Drona had to send his son Ashwathama to intervene. He stops them and says,"Acharya had commanded this fight to stop. Both of you are equally capable. Your violent aggression is inappropriate. So stop it now". After they stopped, Guru Drona stood up and announced, "O audience! Now behold the skill of Arjuna, the son of Kunti and Indra. He is dearer to me than my own son, who has mastered all weapons". Thereafter, on the instructions of the Acharya, the young warrior Arjun appeared on the stage wearing gloves made of monitor lizard skin, carrying a quiver full of arrows and a bow. With the entry of Arjun, the entire stage was filled with joy and happiness. Various Musical instruments and conchs started playing everywhere for Arjun, and people with excitement started praising him, saying he was the brilliant son of Kunti. He is the youngest son of Pandu. He is the child of Indra, the king of the devatas. He is the protector of the

Kuru dynasty. He is the best of the scholars of weapons. He is the best of the righteous and the virtuous. He is the best treasures of virtue and knowledge". After listening to his praises and cheering, he began showing his skill with the permission of the king and His Guru, Dronacharya. First, he created fire with Agneyastra; then, he extinguished it by creating water with Varunastra. He started a storm with Vayavyastra and created clouds with Parjanyastra; then he created the stones with the Bhaumaastra and the mountains with the Parvatastra; then he became invisible with the help of the Antardhanastra. In a moment, he would become very tall, and in a moment, he would become very small. In one moment, he would appear big on the axle of the chariot, and in the next moment, he would be seen in the middle of the chariot. Then, in the blink of an eye, he would descend to the earth and start displaying his skill in using weapons. In this way, he displayed great skill in handling weapons. Arjuna, skilled in the weapons of sword, bow and mace, showed many tricks and skills. Just when the muscial sound and excitement begin to calm, Karṇa entered the arena with the great envy towards Pandavas.Tall and radianty like a golden tree, his presence was commanding.His limbs resembled that of a lion. His body emitted the divine glow of surya At that time, Karṇa looked around the stage and bowed half-heartedly to Dronacharya and Kripacharya ,as if he did not have much respect for them. Then he turned towards Arjun and arrogantly said, "Kunti Nandan! I will do even more wonderful deeds than what you have done in front of these spectators. So do not be proud of your valour. " Seeing this, Duryodhan's lit up with happiness, as he has found the nectar of life(Amrit). Arjun gets a little tensed as he speaks. Then, after getting permission from Guru Drona, he showed his archery skills to the public, and he performs the same astonishing thing as Arjun in the arena. Thereafter, Duryodhan, along with his brother, embraced Karn happily and said,"Mahabaho! You are welcome." You have come here; it is a great fortune for us. This kingdom of the Kauravas and I are all yours. Enjoy them to your fullest."Then he(Karṇa) presented his desire to have duel with Arjun . Then Arjun replied,"O Karṇa! If ! I defeat you, you will go to the same disgraceful as one who speak or act without being invited"Then Karṇa angrily replied, "Only the weak resort to words. If you are truly brave, speak through your arrows.Today, I will sever your head in front of your guru" Thereafter, Kunti's son Arjun, taking the permission of Acharya Drona, proceeded towards arena. Then, Duryodhan, along with his brothers, embraced Karṇa, who was ready for the battle with his bow and arrow.Kripacharya stepped in and said— "Karṇa! This Kunti Devi's youngest son Arjuna, is the jewel of the Kuru dynasty,In a duel, a prince must face another prince . So, tell us of your parentage,linage and royal heritage.Only then this duel can take place prince" listening this Karṇa 's face become pale seeing this Duryodhan said

"If Arjun does not wish to fight on the battlefield with a person other than the king, then I will anoint Karṇa as the king of Angadesh right now. " Then, the priest, with the order of Duryodhan, performed all the rituals of the Rajyabhisekh and made him the king of the Anga desh. Then Karṇa asked Duryodhan you had give me this kingdom how should I return your favour then Duryodhan replied "I want to have such friendship that would never end" thereafter Karṇa's father Adiratha enters the ground looking for Karṇa, seeing him Karṇa immediately went to him leaving his seat to greet him and to take his blessings. Seeing Adiratha, Bhimsen remembers about Karṇa and how both Karṇa and Duryodhan used to conspired against them and insulted them in childhood so he insulted Karṇa by saying " O Sutaputra! You are not even worthy of death at the hands of Arjuna. You should soon take the whip in your hand; for this is befitting of your family". hearing this this, Karṇa's lips trembled with rage. He looked up toward Surya deva in the sky. At this very time, the mighty Duryodhan furious, jumped up and thundered. "O Vrakodar, you should not say this. Strength is the most important thing among Kshatriyas. If you are strong, you should fight even with a Kshatriya (lower Kshatriya) (or you should fight with Karṇa because he is a friend of me, a Kshatriya). It is very difficult to know the country and the real reason of the origin of warriors and rivers; for example, the Great Vajra came from Dadhichi 's bone marrow. Bhagwan Skanda was born from agni(fire), kritika, Rudra and Ganga. Many great

Brahmins were born in kshatriya families. One of the brahmins is Brahmarishi Vishwamitra, who was born in a kshatriya clan. Our Acharya Drona, the best among all weapon wielders, was born from a pot. Kripacharya was also born from a group of reeds in the family of Maharishi Gautam. I also know how you were born and how come a warrior who as majestics could belong to suta clan. How can a person born in a Suta clan be as radiant as the Sun, who is endowed with such Kshatriya qualities and who beautifies the battlefield? With his physical strength and the help of an obedient friend like me, King Karṇa will conquer not only his country but the entire earth".With that declaration, Duryodhan embraced Karna and left the arena. The Pandav along with the elders also deported their residence

<u>Note</u>: The scholars and TV serials show depicts this event of the tournament through a superficial and distorted lens that Karṇa was discriminated based on his caste, and he wasn't allowed to duel with Arjun this is caste discrimination. No, its not a caste discrimination it's a rule that only a prince will fight another prince and if we see it in today context that a man born in rich family which owns a huge industry then that person will see the Man of the other rich family as his competitor not their manager, hence Karṇa was never been discriminated because of caste.

PANCHAL WAR

After the tournament ended, Dronacharya having seen seen both the the Pandavas and Kauravs become proficient in the art of the weapons, decided that the time had come for Guru Dakshina and decided to summon his students.He summoned all his student and said, "Disciples! Capture Panchala king Drupada in the war and bring him to me. May you be blessed. This will be the best Guru dakshina for me. "All the student accepted the command and quickly readied their chariot for war. Thereafter, Duryodhana, Karṇa, the mighty Yuyutsu, Dushasan, Vikarṇa, Jalasandh, Sulochana and many other valiant prince marched toward the Panchal country saying. "I will fight first, I will fight first" and while beating the inhabitants of that place, they began assaulting the capital of the king Drupada .But Draupad, a fierce warrior and once a classmate of Droancharya, was no ordinary king.On seeing his city under attack, he emerged with his brother-fully armouredand ready for battle.Arjun, observing afar,told Dronacharya "Gurudev! After they(kaurav) show their prowess, we will attack Panchala. I believe that these people cannot defeat Panchalraj"Following this Arjun and Pandavs halted outside the city while the battle between Kaurav and Draupad began. King Drupada attacked them from all sides, spread a huge net of arrows, and stunned the Kaurava army. Although King Drupada, who showed agility in the war, was sitting on the chariot and showering arrows alone, due to extreme fear, the Kauravas started believing him to be many. Drupada's fierce arrows started flying in all directions. Seeing his victory, thousands of musical instruments like conch, bheri and mridanga started playing simultaneously in the houses of the Panchalas. The Panchala soldiers, endowed with great self-confidence, started roaring. Along with that, the loud twang of their bowstrings started echoing in the sky. At that time, Duryodhan, ViKarna, Subahu, Dirghlochara and Dushasan were filled with great anger and started raining arrows. Drupada got severely injured and immediately inflicted great pain on all the armies. He moved around like a wheel of fire and started scorching Duryodhan, ViKarna, Mahabalo, Karna, and their armies with arrows. He shot ten piercing arrows at Dushasana, twenty at ViKarna and thirty very sharp arrows at Shakuni making him injured After this, Draupad separately struck the joints of all the limbs of Karna and Duryodhana with his twenty-eight arrows. He wounded Subahu with five arrows and also shot other warriors with many kinds of arrows, then roared. Thus roaring with rage, Panchal king Drupada, cut off the bows, chariots, horses and colourful flags of the enemies. After that, all the Panchal soldiers started roaring like lions. Then all the residents of that city attacked the Kauravas and started raining pestles and sticks on them like rain clouds. The mighty warriors of Hastinapur were defeated and Humiliated-even a Karna who is even glorified by modern tv serials and scholars as a peerless warrior.

पाञ्चालशरभित्राङ्गो भयमासाद्य वै वृषः कणों रथादवप्लुत्य पलायनपरोऽभवत्

Karna's entire body was wounded by the arrows of Panchal King Drupada. He got frightened and jumped from the chariot and ran away

(Adiparva,sambhavparva,chap 127, shlok 25)

. Seeing kauravs fleeing from Panchal, Arjun, along with other Pandavs, enters into the Panchal and then, listening to the roar of the enemies, Arjuna, along with his brothers, advances with great speed, the rattling sound of the chariot echoing in all directions. Listening to the chariots' sound, the Panchal army gathered together and surrounded the Pandavas from all sides. This made Bhimsen angry. He went inside the elephant army alone with his mace and started killing them. He started hitting elephants on their heads with his mace, and due to the head being split by Bhimasena's mace, those huge elephants, as big as mountains, were falling on the ground like mountains, with blood gushing out due to the blow of the thunderbolt (with their wings cut off). Bhima, the elder brother of Arjuna, destroyed the elephants, horses and chariots. He killed the foot soldiers and charioteers. Just as a cowherd drives away animals in the forest with a stick, in the same way, Bhimasen started chasing the charioteers and elephants.

At the same time, Arjun went directly to Draupad along with his army and started showing arrows, destroying horses, chariots, and herds of elephants from all sides of the battlefield. He then spread such a huge net of arrows, enveloping and mesmerizing them, making it impossible for the Panchal army to see Arjun from where he is showering arrows on them. Therefore, King Draupad, along with his brother, Satyajit, attacked Arjun with great speed, but Arjun covers him with heavy shower of arrows. But somehow King Draupad saving himself from those arrows went near to Arjun with intention to capture him. When Satyajit saw this, he launched a direct attack on Arjun; thus, their battle became as extreme as the battle between devas and asuras. Then Arjuna wounded Satyaji with ten piercing arrows by striking him forcefully. Then, Panchal warrior Satyajit also quickly struck a hundred arrows and troubled Arjun. Covered with a shower of arrows, the great Arjun, who was very swift, cleaned the bowstring and started shooting arrows, and after cutting Satyajit's bow, he attacked King Drupada.Then Satyajit took another powerful bow and attacked Arjuna along with his horse, chariot and charioteer. Getting wounded by Satyajit's arrows, Arjun became angry, and Arjuna destroyed Satyajit's horse, flag, bow, fist and both the power guard and charioteer. Thus, after the bow was repeatedly broken and the horses were killed, Satyajit fled from the battlefield. Seeing him turned away from the battle, King Drupada of Panchala began to shower arrows with great speed on Arjuna. Then Arjuna began a heavy battle with him. Then Arjun cut the bow and flag of the Panchala king. Then he injured his charioteer with five arrows. Then, abandoning the broken bow, when King Draupad was about to pick up another bow and quiver, Arjuna drew his sword from the sheath and roared. Then he jumped on his chariot and put his sword on King Draupad's neck. Seeing their king captured,the panchala soldiers fled in all directions. Thus, he captures King Draupad along with his ministers and gifts him to his Guru Dronacharya as a Guru Dakshina. Then he said to Draupad with restrained irony, "Once, you mocked me and broke our bond of friendship in your court. But now, I have conquered you. Do you still refuse my friendship?". ashamed Draupad apologized, than Dronacharya happily forgaves him and gave half of Panchaal back to him.

Note: Modern tv serials and left leaning scholars often portray Karṇa as the "greatest warrior"who never lost a battle.But Vyas's Mahabharat clearly state otherwise.In this Panchala war, Karna fled from battlefield even though he had his divine armor . Meanwhile Arjun effortlessly captured Draupad and fulfilled his Guru's wish

CONSPIRACY

After a year had passed, Dhritarashtra consecrated Yudhisthira, the son of Pandu, as the princely king because of his virtues such as patience, steadfastness, tolerance, kindness, simplicity and unwavering It was a gesture to demonstrate the royal family righteousness before the people. By this time Arjun had mastered the art of weaponry under Dronacharya . Impressed by his loyaltyand skills, guru Dronacharya gave him knowledge of secret divine astras.Similarly, Bhimsen had also mastered the arts of paces, swords, and chariots under Balram Ji. Nakula and Sahadev became great scholars of Niti Shastra under Dronacharya. After completing their education,Arjun and Bhimsen,embark on a Vijay yatra and extended Hastnapur's boundaries . In their yatra, they conquered many kingdoms,including the those of the Yavans, which even King Pandu failed to subdue. Arjun also killed king Vipul of sauvira, who was as powerful as Gandharvas along with his general Dattamitra. Apart from this, Arjuna, riding a single chariot alongside Bhima, he crushed the armies of the eastern direction and defeated ten thousand charioteers .Thus, he returned to Hastinapur not just as warrior but as a true "Dhananjaya" - conqueror of wealth and kingdom. But these of Pandavs ignited envy and fear in Duryodhan's heart. He become anxious and began plotting to kill pandavs .Togethe with Karṇa and shakuni, he devised a wicked plan to burned the Pandavs alive along with their mother.

ततःसुबलपुत्रस्तु राजा दुर्योधनश्च है। दुश्शासनश्च कर्णश्च दुष्टं मन्त्रममन्त्रयन ॥ १ ॥
धृतर मैं कौरव्यमनुज्ञाप्य धृतराष्ट्रं नराधिपम्। दहने तु सपुत्रायाःकुन्त्या बुद्धिमकारयन

Thereafter Shakuni, the son of Subala, King Duryodhana, Dussasana and Karṇa took a wicked secret counsel (among themselves)After taking permission from Dhritarashtra,they devised to burn Mata Kunti in fire along with her sons

(Adiparva, Jatugriha parv , chap 140, shlok 1&2)

They went to King Drithrasthra and expressed their insecurity regarding the Pandav's rising fame. They urged him to send Pandav along with Mata Kunti to Varnavrat where they would execute their plan.Initially King Drithrasthra objected, saying, "King Pandu, following his dharma, always respects everyone, and especially he respected and honored me. he used to tell me every day that 'This kingdom is yours'. His son Yudhisthira was equally pious Like him. Pandavas are endowed with excellent qualities, famous in the whole world and very dear to the ancestors. Pandu had taken care of all the ministers and soldiers. He also took special care of the maintenance of their grandsons.

Then how come we take away their ancestor kingdom by force when they had so much support? King Pandu ruled his people very well. If we go against his sons, then people will surely revolt and kill us for the Sake of their prince."Listening to this, Duryodhan replied, "Father! I too had anticipated this flaw (of being against the people) in my heart and keeping this in mind, I had already honored all the people with money and respect. "Duryodhan again insisted the king to sent pandas to varnavrat immediately,so he could unsurp the throne before their return .King drithasthra hesitated: "I too have considered this, but it is sinful so I didn't dare spoke it aloud. Beside Bhishma, Vidur, Drona and Kripacharya will never allow pandavas to go there without any reason" then Duryodhan assured him "Father! Bhishma is always the mediator, Drona's son Ashwatthama is on my side, and Dronacharya will also be on the side where his son is - there is no doubt about this at all. On the side where these two are, Kripacharya will also be on the same side. He will never be able to leave his brother-in-law Dronacharya. Vidur is also bound by our financial bondage; Vidur is secretly bound by the affection of our enemies. He alone will not be able to create obstacles for the benefit of the Pandavas. Therefore, you should send the Pandavas along with their mother to Varnavata without any worry and make such arrangements so that they can leave today itself. "Listening to this king, Drithrasthra remembers his minister's words and assures Duryodhan that he will order Pandav to leave for Varnavrat.

Thereafter,Duryodhan , Karna and Shakuni bribed the minister to spread rumours about the beauty of Varnavrat.Its famous Shiva festival, and its prosperity. The idea was to entice Pandavas into going there without suspicion. Soon , the minister began talking about Varnavrat being the most delightful city and that a grand festival was taking place. Hearing this, Pandavas expressed their desire to there.So, Dritharasthra appraoched them and said "Ohh, sons, you all have learned scriptures and also gained mastery in weapons.The city of Varnavrat is hosting the greatest fair in all the Aryavarta.Go there, enjoy the festivities, and live like the devas." Yudhishthira saw through the deception, but knowing himself to be helpless, he accepted his wish, sayin "Very good". 'Then, with poor feeling, he said to every minister and king, "All of you, please be happy and give us your blessings. Your blessings will help us prosper, and sin will not be able to control us."Then, everyone blessed them and prayed for their well-being. Thus, Pandav started their preparation for leaving Hastinapur. Meanwhile, Duryodhan and Karṇa secretly summoned Purochan, their loyal minister and order him to construct palace made of lac and other inflammable substances.They instructed him "Treat the Pandav kindly, win their trust and when they are comfortable, burn the house during the night".Therefore, he immediately went to the varnavrat and beagn executing the plan. As The Pandavas prepare to leave , they took blessing from grandfather Bhishma Dhritarashtra,Drona, Kripacharya, Vidura and the other elders. During the farewell, Mahatma Vidur warned them about the Duryodhan conspiracy through sign language. Understanding the warning, the Pandavs (Pandavs) became extremely cautious and went out of Hastinapur on their chariot towards Varnavrat. Upon reaching Varnavrat, they were warmly greeted by Purochan and escorted to a newly built palace. After settling, they(Pandavs and Mata Kunti) went to everyone's house from Brahmin to shudra to meet them and to learn of the city. For a year , Purochan served them attentively, they (Pandav) also pretended to trust him.During , this time , Vidur had secretly sent a minor to dig a tunnel from palace to the forest.When the preparation were complete Pandavs, along with Mata Kunti, escaped through the tunnel and burned the palace along with Purochan and his servants. Then they crossed the river on the boat prepared by Mahatma Vidor and went into the dark forest to fake their death in order to hide themselves. Meanwhile, when King Drithrastha and his son received this news, they pretended to be sad and went to Varnavrta to take away their remaining to perform last rites at the bank of the river Ganga. During the ritual of the last rites, Bhishma get overcome with sorrow .Seeing this, Mahatma Vidur quietly informed him about escape of Pandavas from the burning palace. Listening this, Bhishma holds his hands and takes him away from kauravas and asked about pandav then Mahatma vidur said "Dhritarashtra, Shakuni, Karṇa and King Duryodhan plotted to burn the Pandavas.I had a tunnel a built and rescued them, when the time is right, they will return and reclaimwhat is theirs " relieved Bhishma calmed himself and then returned to Hastinapur. Meanwhile, in the forest, The Pandavs faced many hardship. They encountered rakshas siblings Hidimbi and Hidimbasur. Bhimsen killed Hidimbasur and married Hidimbi,who later gave birth to Ghatochkacha. Due to his Rakshas heritage, he grew up instantly And vowed to serve pandavs whenever they would summon him and he taking their blessing , he went to the north direction along with his mother. The Pandavs then traveled to Ekchakra, where they lived disguised as Brahmins and in the Brahmin's house. One day, Mata Kunti overheard grief of the Brahmin family regarding the sacrifice one of their family members to Bakasur for the sake of the town.To save the family, she sent Bhimsen. Then, Bhimsen,on the order of Kunti, went to the demon's cave and killed him, liberating the town from the demon's fear.Thereafter,they continued to live in Ekachakra. Until they heard news of the grand swayamvar being held in Panchal. On their way to Panchal, they encountered Gandharva King Chitrangad, whom Arjun defeated using agneyastra. Impressed the Gandharva king befriended him, and taught him Gandharva vidya in exchange for agneyastra.

Note: Tv serials and scholars claim that Karṇa disagreed with the plan to burn Pandavas,prtraying him as morally superior. However, Vyas's Mahabharat clearly shows that Karna was one of the main conspirator behind this sinister plot.

Swayamvar

During the event of Lakshagraha, King Draupad who had once been captured by Pandavs, and had received onl;y half his kingdom from Dronacharya out of mercy, was filledwith sorrow and humiliation.Angry and determinedto take revenge, he visited the ashrams of the Brahma rishis seeking a ways to kill Drona. At one such ashram, he met Rishi Yaja, whom he convinced to perform a yagya to produce a son who could kill Drona. Then, together, they gathered the required items and started the yagya. At the end of the Yagya, Rishi offers the ritualistic oblations to the Draupad's wife, but she refuses to take it, saying, "O Brahman!I am not prepared. My face is smeared with betel leaf and divine perfumes.I must wash and purify myself before touching the sacred offering . "This made Rishi Yag angry, and he offered that ritualistic oblation directly into the fire. From the flames a prince emerged,radiant as a sun, wearing a crown and armor, and armed with sword, arrow and bow .He roared like a lion and immedlately buarded a great chariot,appearing as if ready for war. Seeing this, Panchal cheered with joy. Then Some invisible Mahabhoot echoed- "This prince will remove the fear of the Panchalas and increase their fame. He will remove the grief of King Drupada kill Dronacharya."Soon after, a virgin girl appeared from the same sacrificial altar, who was called Panchali. She was very beautiful and fortunate. Every part of her body was worth seeing. Her black eyes were big. Her complexion was dark. Her eyes looked like the petals of a blooming lotus. Her hair was black and curly. Her nails were prominent and red. Her eyebrows were very beautiful. She appeared as if Goddess Durga herself had appeared in human form. A fragrance like that of a blue lotus was emanating from her body, and a pleasant smell was spreading all around. She had assumed an extremely beautiful form.The akashvani (voice from the sky) declared: "The name of this girl is Krishna(Draupadi). She is the best and most beautiful among all the girls and has appeared to bring destruction upon the Kshatriyas."Then, Rishi Yajja performed their naming ritual and named the boy"Dhrishthadyumna" and the girl "Draupadi". This is how King Draupad got twin children.Though Dristhadyumna ahd been born for Dronacharya's death. Dronacharya demonstrating the greatness of Dharma, accepted him as his disciple and taught him the art of warfare . Later, King Draupad approached Rishi Yaja asking for the the best groom for his daughter then Rishi replied "The most worthy groom is Arjuna. Though the world believes the Pandavas are dead, I assure you—they are alive and will come if you hold a grand swayamvar" . Overjoyed, King Draupad announced the swayamvar, to be held on the auspicious Ekadashi of bright fortnight of the month of Pausha, under the Rohini Nakshatra. Then King Draupad started the preparation of the swayamvar. Due to his keen eagerness to make Arjun his daughter's groom, he made such a strong bow that no one could bend but Arjun. The king also built an artificial sky machine (which kept rotating in the sky at a high speed). He got a target of the same size made and placed over the hole of that machine. After everything was prepared, he finally announced the task of the Grand swayamvar: "The brave man who will string this bow and pierce the target with these presented arrows through the hole in the instrument shall marry my daughter". When the day arrived , king and prince from across aryavarta gathered in panchala.even Shree Krishna, Balaram and other Yadav warrior came Many great sages and saints also came to see the swayamvar. Kaurav ,led by Duryodhan alsoarrived, bringing Karna with them.The city was adorned like a bride. Garlands hung from every corner, fragrances of sandalwood and incense filled the air, and music from hundreds of instruments enchanted the crowd. Everyone—sages, nobles, and commoners alike—assembled to witness the great event.Thereafter,Draupadi, adorned in resplendent attire and jewelry, holding a golden-embroidered garland, entered the arena alongside Dhrishtadyumna. When the sound of the musical instruments died down and there was silence in the Swayamvar Sabha, then, according to the custom, Dhrishtadyumna stood in the middle of the arena, taking Draupadi with him and announced— "O kings of the world who have gathered here! All of you (pay attention), listen to me. This is the bow, these are the arrows, and this is the target. All of you should pierce the target through the hole of that machine with the five sharp arrows that you have released in the sky and bring it down. I am telling the truth, I am not lying - the one who is of the best family, has a good looks and is blessed with great strength and will perform this great deed, today my sister Krishna will be his wife. "He then pointed out the great king present , including "Duryodhana, Samudrasena Durvishaha, Durmukh, Dushpradharshana, Vivinshati, ViKarṇa, Saha, Jalasandh Duhshasana, Yuyutsu, Vayuvega, Bhimavegarava, Ugrayudha, Paundrava Balaki, Karakayu, Virocana, Kundaka, Chitrasena, Suvarcha, Kali Kanakadhvaja, Nandaka, Bahushali, Tuhunda and Vikata- and lots more".The Pandavas, disguised as Brahmins, also entered silently and took their seats among the Brahmin assembly. Shri Krishna, on seeing them, whispered to Balarama, "Brother, look! The Pandavas are alive, hidden among the Brahmins" Thereafter the swayamvar begans, one by one every king & warrior tried to lift the bow, but none could lift it. Even the great and fierce warriors like Shishupal Jarashangha, Shalya, Duryodhan, and even **Karṇa** couldn't lift that bow. When all the kings turned their backs on the task of stringing the bow, then the Arjuna stood up from the midst of the Brahmin group. When the great Brahmins saw Arjuna, who was as tall as Indra's flag, getting up and going towards his bow, they started praising him. Then Arjun went in front of the bow, and then he bowed down to Bhagwan Mahadev and meditating Shree Krishna in his mind, he picked up the bow.

यत् पार्थिवै रुक्मसुनीथवक्कैःराधेयदुर्योधनशल्यशाल्वैः
तदा धनुर्वेदपरैर्नसिंहैः। कृतं न सज्यं महतोऽपि यत्नात्
तदर्जुनो वीर्यवतां सदर्प स्तदैन्द्रिरिन्द्रावरजप्रभावः
सज्यं च चक्रे निमिषान्तरेण शरांश्च जग्राह दशार्धसंख्यान ॥

And then he took those 5 arrows in his hand and shoot them and In no time the target suddenly fell on the earth from the hole of the instrument. At that time, the target, which was tied to the machine, broke into pieces, and there was a loud sound of joy in the sky. The hall was filled with even more joy and noise. Thousands of Brahmins (filled with joy) started waving their clothes there (as if they were waving the victory flag of Arjuna), then those kings (who were unable to hit the target and had accepted defeat) started making hue and cry from all sides. Flowers were raining from all sides from the sky in that theatre. The musicians started playing trumpets, etc., with hundreds of parts. Sutas and Magadhans started singing praises there in a sweet tone.

Thus, King Draupad become very happy and orders his army to protect him.

Seeing Arjuna,, having pierced the target and fallen on the ground, Draupadi, holding a beautiful white flower garland in her hand, went near Kuntikumar, smiling softly. Even for those who had seen her form many times, she appeared new every day. That Draupadi, appeared to be laughing even without laughing. Even without speaking, she seemed to be communicating only through her eyes. Going near, Arjun, ignoring all the kings gathered there, she suddenly put the garland around Arjun's neck and stood there politely.

Then, after winning the swayamvar, Arjun, along with Draupadi and his brothers, went out of the arena

But the humiliated kings, including Karna and Shalya, rose in fury. Enraged that a Brahmin had won the challenge, they charged toward King Drupada, weapons drawn..

When Drupada saw so many kings approaching in anger and with their bows in hand, hegot terrified and went to the Brahmins for protection. Then, Arjun and Bhimsen ,stepped forward. Then Arjun, to fight them, took the bow and arrow from which he hit the target, and Bhimsen uprooted a tree and used it as a weapon. This made those Kshatriyas even more angry, and they started attacking them. Then, among that warrior, Karna directly went on attacking Arjun. But to his amazement (Karṇa), Arjuna counter his arrows with arrows and hit him with a fierce arrow which make him (Karṇa) lose his senses.

This makes Karṇa frightened, and to save both his life and reputation said, "O Brahmin! I am (very) satisfied with your strength in the war. There is no sign of fatigue or sadness in you, and it seems as if you have conquered all the weapons and have taken them under your control. (I am very happy to see your success.)

Viprashiromane! Are you an idol of Dhanurveda? Or Parshuram? are you Indra himself or Lord Vishnu in person who never loses his glory?

Then Arjun simply replies he is none of them but just a normal Brahmin. Then, due to fear and respect toward the brahmins, he abandons the battle. At the same time, Bhimsen fought with Shalya, and with minimum effort, he lifted Shalya and threw him on the Ground. The Defeat of Karṇa and Shalya created fear among the warriors; they gave up their will to kill King Draupad and returned to their respective homes. After the king leaves, Pandavs and Draupadi take blessings from King Draupad, and leave for their home along with a group of Brahmins. When they went to their hut, Mata Kunti was doing the chores. Then with excitement they said "mother! We have won a prize . "From inside the hut, Kunti, unaware of what it was, replied:

" you should share that among yourself" When she emerged and saw Draupadi, she was stunned. Realizing the implication of her words, she was filled with guilt and confusion. She consulted Yudhishthira, who understood her intent and, observing that all his brothers were attracted to Draupadi, remembered the words of Veda vyasa and declared that Draupadi would become the wife of all five Pandavas. Then, both Draupadi and his brothers, along with Mata Kunti, agreed with him. Soon after, Shri Krishna and Balarama visited the Pandavas, congratulated them, and left discreetly to avoid suspicion about their identities. At the same time,Dhrishtadyumna, who had secretly followed the Pandavas, reported everything to King Drupada. The king sent his purohit to invite the Pandavas to the palace for a feast. They accepted and were warmly welcomed.

After the feast, Drupada asked Yudhishthira:"Tell me, noble one, your true identity and lineage." Yudhisthir revealed"We are the sons of King Pandu. We survived the Lakshagriha and now live in hiding.". Then King Draupad was overjoyed. But when Yudhishthira said that Draupadi would marry all five brothers, the king was shocked and conflicted.

. He asked Mata Kunti about this, and Mata Kunti, with guilt, said that she had ordered them about this; thus, it made King Draupad more worried. Then he again said, "Kunti's son! You, Kuntidevi and my son Dhrishtadyumna - all of them should decide together and tell us what should be done. We will do that tomorrow at the right time. "

That evening, as they sat in confusion, Sage Vedavyasa arrived. All rose to greet him and offered him a golden seat and started the discussion,but didn't come at any conclusion. This make Maa Kunti more worried and anxious and she assumed herself to be the root cause of this problem and asked the sage about her guilt then the sage replied "oh Kunti! you aren't guilty of anything" the sage then said to Drupada: "There is a secret in this marriage, which I will not tell in front of everyone. You go alone and listen to it from me. And also in the manner and reason for which it has been said to be by Sanatan Dharma and how Kunti's son Yudhishthira has propounded its conformity to Dharma, considering it, it is undoubtedly proved that this marriage is by Dharma. "

Therefore the sage Veda Vyas got up from his seat and went inside the royal palace, holding the hand of King Drupada. There, he told him about the secret about Pandav's marriage with Draupadi.

Once, the 5 Indra —Indra, Vishvabhuk, Bhoothdhama, Shibi, and Shanti—were cursed for their ego and held captive by Bhagwan Rudra. When they realized their folly, they begged forgiveness. Mahadev prophesied that they would be born as the Pandavas through the ansha of different devtas and the Swarga Lakshmi (not the goddess Lakshmi- wife of Shree Vishnu, but her partial incarnation) would incarnate as their wife. That Swarga Lakshmi was none other than Draupadi, born from fire.

Thus, the Pandavas, who were Indras earlier, have appeared. This divine Draupadi is the same swarga Lakshmi, who has already been appointed as their wife. Maharaj! If the gods had not cooperated in this task, then how could such a divine woman have appeared from the land of the Upvedi through this yajna ceremony of yours, whose form is spreading light like the sun and the moon and whose fragrance keeps spreading till the night of the night?

After hearing this, Vedavyasa gave divine vision to King Draupada. The king saw the Pandavas in their celestial forms as Indras and Draupadi as Swarga Lakshmi. He was amazed and overjoyed.

Thus, he gave his blessings and ordered the wedding to be arranged. Thereafter, the priest, who was well versed in the Vedas and who knew how to chant mantras, placed a burning fire on the altar and offered oblations in it by chanting mantras. He summoned Yudhiṣṭhira and tied him to Draupadi. A priest, having full knowledge of the Vedas, got the couple married and made them circumnavigate the fire, then (by performing other rituals prescribed in the scriptures) completed their marriage. In this way, Draupadi marries each Pandav on different days.

Thus, King Draupad gave them a lot of jewels, pearls, horses, etc, as a gift, and they (Pandav and Mata Kunti) started living there in the Panchal kingdom in the King's palace.

37

DISCUSSION

Soon after the Swayamvar, news spread across Aryavarta that the Pandavas were alive. And the one who hit the target with that invincible bow and defeated the Karṇa along with other warriors is none other than Arjun himself. The brahmin who had thrown King Shalya on the ground is the Mighty Bhimsen himself. The rest of the 3 Brahmins who were standing beside these 2 were Yudhisthir, Nakul and Sahadev. The citizens of Hastinapur rejoiced upon hearing the news. But at the same time, they also remembered the burning of the Lakshagriha. Many citizens, ministers, and rishis condemned King Dhritarashtra and even Bhishma Pitamaha for allowing the conspiracy to happen.Meanwhile, in the royal court of Hastinapur, Duryodhana, Karna, and Shakuni were burning with rage. They feared that the Pandavas, now backed by the powerful King Drupada and Lord Krishna, would soon return with massive support. A royal meeting was immediately convened to discuss how to handle this crisis. Where shakuni said "Before the Pandavas gain strength through new alliances, we must strike first. Let us send an army to Panchala and either defeat them or capture them by force."Then, the Prince of Bahik Kingdom Burishrava, interrupting him, said,"No one here can defeat Arjuna or Bhimsen. And Yudhishthira is wise beyond his years. If we attack now, we will be destroyed. Instead, we should make peace—

temporarily—and divide the kingdom to keep our grip on power.," King Drithrasthra agreed with him and expressed his pseudo-love for the Pandavs.The thought of the Pandavs marrying Draupadi and,now Drithrasthra agreeing with courtiers, made Duryodhan both sad and angry.So,he left the court along with Karṇa, Shakuni and his Brothers. That night, he and Karṇa, went to the King's room. Both of them said to King Drithrasthra, "Maharaj! We cannot tell you any of your faults in front of Courtiers. We are alone right now; that is why we are saying this. What do you want to do? Respected father! You have started considering the progress of your enemies as your progress, and in front of courtiers, you praise our enemies a lot. 'Father, at this moment it will be best for us to destroy Pandavs before they destroy us" Then King Dritrasthra replied, "Son! I, too, want to do the same thing as you both want, but I do not want to let my feelings be visible to courtiers, especially Vidur, even through my appearance. That is why I especially tell about the qualities of the Pandavas in front of Vidur, so that he cannot tease my feelings even by a gesture. Duryodhana and Karṇa! Whatever work you both think is necessary to be done at this time, please tell me quickly." Duryodhan then suggested creating enmity between Pandav and King Draupad and killing Bhimsen by deceit, as he was the bone marrow of the Pandavs. After presenting his ideas to his father, he then asked Karna for his opinion on this matter. Then, Karṇa said, "Duryodhan! I think your advice is not right. Kuruvardhan! The Pandavas cannot be controlled by any such means. Brave one! Earlier, you tried to drown the Pandavas by using many secret means, but you could not control them. O King! When they were children and lived here with you, no one was in their favour, and even then, you could not succeed in killing them. Now, it is not even possible to create divisions among them. Those who are (unanimously) devoted to the same wife cannot have any conflict with each other. It is impossible to separate Draupadi from them by creating a rift because when the Pandavas were poor and miserable due to being alms-eaters, Draupadi had chosen them at that time; now that they have become wealthy and live in clean and beautiful clothes, why would she be indifferent to them now?It is a common tendency in women to be attracted to many men, and Draupadi already has this advantage by living with the Pandavas. So, no discrimination can be created in her mind.Similarly, King Draupad,will never take your side no matter what you give him, and his son Drishtadhumyna follows his father just like a shadow follows the body; thus, taking him on our side is impossible. Thus, the only way left is to attack them now with full force before they get a strong and gathered army. We must hurry and crush the Panchal army with our huge fourfold army and quickly bring Pandavs here as captives before Shree Krishna gets there with his Yadu army to help them to take their kingdom back from you. Hence, you must defeat with power and take over this entire Earth." On hearing Karna's word, King Drithrasthra praised him and said,

"Karṇa! You are extremely intelligent, knowledgeable in weapons and bring joy to the Suta clan. Such a powerful statement is worthy of you. "He then ended the conversation, saying he would discuss the matter with the ministers the next day.The next day in the court, Dhritarashtra asked his ministers for their opinions. Bhishma suggested making peace and giving the Pandavas half the kingdom to undo the injustice done to them. Guru Dronacharya supported Bhishma and said the same. Seeing Bhishma and Dronacharya take Pandav's side, Karna insulted them, saying,

" Maharaj! Bhishmaji and Dronacharya always receive money and respect from you. You consider them your close friends and take their advice in all matters. Yet if they do not advise for your good, then what can be more surprising than this? How can a person who advises with a guilty heart, hiding the evil intentions of his heart, achieve the desired welfare of the virtuous people who have faith in him? O King! You are wise, so by thinking in this way, you should understand the saintliness and sinfulness of your ministers. You should also know who has advised with a tainted heart and who with a faultless heart."

This made Dronacharya angry, and he said to Karṇa. "O wicked one! We know why you say such things. The hatred that you have accumulated in your heart for the Pandavas is the reason why you are finding faults in my words. I am telling you something very beneficial. If anything contrary to that is done, then the Kauravas will soon be destroyed - this is my opinion" Then King Drithrashras asked Mahatma Vidur about this, and Vidur said, "O King! These well-wishing relatives of yours must tell you things that are undoubtedly beneficial. But you do not want to listen, that is why even the beneficial things told by them are not accepting it. Maharaj! Even after a lot of thinking, I do not see any person in this court who is superior in intelligence and thinking power to these two brave great men(Bhishma and Drona). Both of them are superior in age, intelligence and knowledge of scriptures and have equal respect. Hence, you must listen to them instead of Duryodhan & Karṇa. They (Duryodhan, Karṇa & shakuni) are foolish and unrighteous so you must'n listen to them".

King Drithrasthra agrees with him(Vidur) and sends him as a messenger to Pandavs in Panchal. When Vidura reached Panchala, the Pandavas and King Drupada welcomed and honored him with a golden seat and the best food and drinks. He greeted them and conveyed Dhritarashtra's message. The king's decision to give half the kingdom to Yudhishthira made both the Pandavas and King Drupada happy. They accepted the decision and went to Hastinapur along with Vidura. Later, in Hastinapur, King Dhritarashtra gave half the kingdom to the Pandavas. But seeing Duryodhana and Karṇa unhappy, he gave them Khandavprastha—a land which was once the capital of great kings like Yayati and Nahusha, but now had become barren—as their capital.

Still, both the Pandavas and Shree Krishna happily accepted it and went there after the Rajyabhishek (coronation) ceremony. Upon arriving, Shree Krishna summoned Devraj Indra and requested him to build a grand city. On Indra's command, Vishwakarma, the celestial architect, built a stunning and unique city. With Indra's grace and Shree Krishna's guidance, Yudhishthira named it Indraprastha. He became its king, Arjuna and Bhimsen took charge of its defense, while Nakula and Sahadeva handled agriculture and health ministries respectively.

Note: Karṇa was not a great man, as often shown in television and literature. His heart was full of ego and hatred. He insulted the most respected elders— Bhishma and Dronacharya—and made horrible remarks not just on Draupadi but on all women. This clearly showed his deep hatred for the Pandavas.

CONSPIRACY OF GAMBLING

 After taking Indraprastha as their capital, the pandavs killed many enemies of kuru vamsha by the order of King Drithrasthra and Bhishma and made the their boundaries free of enemies After Taking shelter of Dharmaraja Yudhishthira, everyone began to live happily, just as a soul lives happily, just as a soul lives lives happily after receiving a good body as a result of good deeds. The people were not only satisfied with his royal duties but also always happy because they had respect and devotion towards him. There was devotion towards the king because whatever was dear to the people, King Yudhishthir always fulfilled it through his actions. Thereafter, after a few days, Arjun said to Shri Krishna, "Krishna! It is very hot. Come, let us go to take a bath in the Yamuna". After giving this advice and taking Yudhishthira's permission, Arjuna and Shri Krishna went there with their friends. While they relaxed on the bank of of River Yamuna, Agni dev came to them disguised as Brahmin and asked them to help him consume the khandav forest because the snake king Takshak was a friend of Devraj Indra, and whenever he tried to burn it, Indra always neutralizes him with rainwater. Then Arjun said "O Lord. I have many divine and excellent weapons with which I can fight not just one but many Vajradha wielders. But I do not have a bow commensurate with my strength, which could withstand my speed when I try to fight in the battlefield. Besides this, to continue shooting arrows quickly, I would need so many arrows that they would never end. And I do not have a chariot powerful enough to carry the arrows as per my wish. Similarly, Lord Krishna does not have any weapon comparable to His strength and valour, with which He could kill the serpents and ghosts in battle. "After Arjun said this, Agnidev, adorned with a smoke-like flag, thought of Lokpal Varuna with the desire to see him. Then, knowing that Varuna Deva always resided in water, he immediately appeared before them. On seeing Varun Dev, Agni Dev honoured him and asked him to give the divine chariot and Gandiva bow made by Brahma himself to Arjun and Chakra to Shree Krishna. Varun Dev then fulfilled his request and gave them their respective weapons and, returned to his Loka . After this, Agni dev, along with Arjun and Shree Krishna, went to the Khandav forest and started burning it. Both Arjun and Shree Krishna began killing the wild animals to prevent them from escaping . The huge flames of the blazing fire rose high into the sky and struck great fear in the hearts of the Devatas. Terrified by that flame, the devatas and Maharishis and all the inhabitants of the heavenly world went to Devraj Indra and informed him about the flames After hearing this, Indra went there to investigate. Upon seeing Agni dev burning the khandav forest, he becomes angry and started raining heavily. This began to neutralise the flames. Seeing this Arjun covered the forest with arrows and prevented the rain. This made Indra more angry, and he waged a direct war against them and used his mighty vajra against Arjun. Then he (Arjun) neutralised it with vavyaastra . Meanwhile, ugly beasts, pisash, ghosts, and huge snakes came out from the depths of the forest and started attacking Shree Krishna. Then, Vasudev slashed them with chakra like a chef cuts the vegetables into small pieces . This frightened them and they began running here & there. On the other hand, seeing a battle between Indra and Arjun, all the other devta with their divine battle came to aid Indra and started attacking Arjun and Shree Krishna. Seeing Devta coming with divine weapon, Shri Krishna and Arjun stood up with their bows drawn. Both warriors became angry and started wounding the Devtas with their thunderbolt-like arrows. Devtas tried repeatedly but could not succeed. Their hopes were dashed, and out of fear, they abandoned the battle and went to Indra for refuge. Thereafter, to test Arjun's bravery, Indra started pelting heavy stones at him. But Arjun destroyed it with fierce arrows. Then, Indra in attempt to kill Arjuna, with his two hands uprooted the great peak of Mandar Mountain along with the trees and hurled it at them. Arjuna then broke the mountain peak into thousands of pieces with his swift,straight and flaming arrows. Then the shattered mountain fell on the ground, killing many creatures. When the devatas failed to protect the Khandava forest or extinguish the fire, they turned backs and fled. Then, the mighty-armed Shri Krishna released that released a terrible disc, which shone with brilliance, for the destruction of the remaining beings. Struck by the Chakra, all the small creatures like demons, night-creatures, etc., were shattered into hundreds of pieces and fell into the fire. At that time, the form of Shri Krishna, the omnipotent soul who destroyed vampires, snakes, and demons, appeared very terrifying. All the demons had gathered from all sides, but not one emerged who could defeat Shri Krishna or Arjuna. After the devatas returned, a divine voice from the sky addressed Indra and said,

"Bhagwan Vasudev and Arjun cannot be defeated in any kind of war. You can understand what I am saying. These two are the Reincarnation of Bhagwan Nar & Narayan. They are famous even in heaven. You also know how strong they are. They are undefeated and fierce warriors. They cannot be defeated in war by anyone in the entire world. These two great ancient sages Nara-Narayana are highly revered by the Devtas, demons, Yakshas, Rakshas, Gandharvas, humans, Kinnars(semi divine beings not transgender) and serpents. Hence Indra! It is right for you to go from here with the devtas. Consider this destruction of Khandav forest as an act of destiny. "

 Hearing this divine voice, Devraj Indra accepted it as true and leaving behind his anger and resentment, he returned to Swarga . After this, Shree Krishna and Arjun killed the remaining beings and threw them into the fire. In this way, they satisfied Agni Deva. After being satisfied with the meat, blood and fat of the wild animals, Agni Deva became smokeless as he flew in the sky. His eyes began to shine, his tongue grew bright, and his huge face lit up. His radiant hair stood upwards, his eyes turned red, and he drank the juice of the fat of the creatures. Agni Dev felt very happy and satisfied after receiving food from Shri Krishna and Arjuna as per his desire. He attained great peace. Then Mayasur, the engineer deity of Asuras, came out of the fire to save his life. Seeing that Shree Krishna had raised his cakra to kill him, he approached Arjun and begged for protection. When Arjuna granted him protection, Shree Krishna dropped his intent to kill Mayasura, and even Agnidev spared him. Agnidev, protected by Shri Krishna and Arjun from the attack of Indra, burned the Khandava forest for fifteen days. After the burning of the Khandav forest, Mayasur asks Arjun to accept something in return for saving his life. Arjun refused at first, but then he told him to do whatever Shree Krishna asked. Then he approached Vasudev and asked what to do. Govind ordered him to build an unimaginably magnificent Sabhabhavan (assembly hall) for King Yudhishthira. Afterwards, they went to King Yudhishthira and told him everything. With his permission, Mayasura began constructing the sabhabhavan. Mayasur took 14 months to complete the construction of the sabhabhavan. And after the construction, he informed the King and went to Pataal Lok. King Yudhisthir then settled there with his ministers, and many kings and warriors from all over the world came and greeted him. Then, one day, King

Yudhisthir expressed his desire to do Rajsurya yagya in front of Shree Krishna, and his brother, Shree Krishna, said, "O King! Just now, King Jarasandh has been anointed as the emperor by the kings, surpassing the royal wealth of all those Kshatriya clans, and he is becoming the leader of all the kings by attacking all the cities with his might and valour. Jarasandha prefers the policy of creating division among all the kings while enjoying the middle position. At present, he is the most powerful and great king, and the whole world is under his sole control. Jarasandha has attained a special kind of power by worshipping Mahadevji through intense penance; that is why all those kings have been defeated by him. He wants to perform a yajna by sacrificing the kings. O best of kings! He has almost fulfilled his promise. Till he is alive you can't perform rajsurya yagya you must have to kill him" then Yudhisthir asked "How will we defeat him when even the gods could not defeat him? Shree Krishna replied "Even all the gods and demons cannot defeat him in a war, so in my understanding he should be defeated through arm wrestling. I have policy, Bhimasena has strength, and Arjuna is the protector of both of us; therefore, just as three fires make a sacrifice successful, in the same way, the three of us together will complete the task of killing Jarasandha. When we three meet King Jarasandha in private, he will agree to fight a duel with any one of us; there is no doubt about this. Fearing insult, being eager to fight with the great warrior Bhimasena and being proud of his physical strength, Jarasandha will certainly be ready to fight with Bhimasena. Just as a single Yamaraja is sufficient to destroy the entire universe, in the same way, the mighty Bhimasena is sufficient to kill Jarasandha."

According to the plan, the three disguised themselves as Brahmins and went to Jarasandha's palace. They challenged him to a wrestling match. Jarasandha chose Bhimasena for the duel. In the fierce battle that followed, with the help of Vasudeva, Bhimasena killed Jarasandha and freed the world from his tyranny. Afterward, Jarasandha's son and the kings whom he had imprisoned surrendered to King Yudhishthir. One day, Arjuna, who had already obtained the best bow, two huge and inexhaustible quivers, a divine chariot, a flag and a wonderful assembly hall, said to Yudhishthira, "O King, I have got bow, arms, arrows, valour, a helper like Sri Krishna, land (kingdom and the fort of Indraprastha), fame and strength - all these rare and desired things. Now, I consider it necessary to increase our treasury. I wish to conquer all the kings and collect taxes from them. If you permit, I will set out on the best date, time and constellation to conquer the Northern direction nurtured by Kubera" This made King Yudhishthir and his courtiers very happy. They praised Arjuna for his dedication to the kingdom and to the King. Then, Sage Vyasa gladly instructed Arjuna and the other three Pandavas to go in different directions to conquer kingdoms, so that King Yudhishthir could perform the Rajsuya Yagya. He ordered Arjuna to go north,

Bhimasena to the east, Nakula to the west, and Sahadeva to the south. With the blessings of the King and the sage, the Pandavas began their Digvijaya Yatra (conquest of all directions).

Thus, Arjun went to the North direction with his army, where he, without much effort, conquered bhumpal of Kulinda kingdom. Then, after defeating the Kulindas and the kings of the Kalkuta and Anart countries along with their armies, he continued his campaign. Thereafter, tormenting the enemies, Arjun took Sumandalu as his companion and went on to conquer Shakaldeep and King Prativi.A fierce battle took place between Arjun's soldiers and the kings of Shakaldweepa and the other seven islands. Arjun then conquered those archers and, along with them, attacked Pragjyotishpur. A huge battle occured between Arjun and Bhagdutta, the friend of Indra and the King of Pragjyotishpur, which lasted for 8 days. King Bhagdutta was supported by many warriors from Kirat, China and the coastal regions. In the end, Arjun defeated them and made them submit to Indrasprastha. After conquering Bhagadutta, Arjun, proceeded towards the north, protected by Kubera. Thus, Arjun further conquered the regions named Antargiri, Bahirgiri and Upgiri respectively. Then, after subjugating all the mountains and the kings residing there, he collected wealth from everyone. After pleasing those kings, he, along with them, attacked King Brihanta of Uluk and defeated him. Thereafter defeating Brihanta, he subjugated the Modapur,

Vaamdev, Sudama, Susankul and Uttar Uluk along with their rulers. Then Arjun stayed there and, with the help of his servants, conquered the region called Panchagana. From there, he went to the Senabindu kingdom and conquered all the mountain kings living there and proceeded to the Paurav Kingdom. He had a fierce battle with the Paurav forces and defeated them, along with the seven tribals of dacoits known as "utsavsanket". After this, Dhananjaneya defeated the Kshatriya warriors of Kashmir and King Lohit, along with ten allied groups. Thereafter, many Kshatriya warriors like Trigarta, Darva and Kokanad came to seek shelter under Kuntinandan Arjuna from all sides. After this, Dhananjay conquered the beautiful Abhisari city and also defeated King Rochman of Urga in the battle. Thereafter, Arjun attacked the beautiful city of Singhpur, protected by King Chitrayudha, and conquered it in the war. After this, Arjun attacked with his whole army and crushed the armies of the Suhma and Chola countries. After that Arjun caused a great massacre and subdued the Bahika warriors. Arjuna with a powerful army defeated the Kambojas and Dardas. He also conquered Param Kamboja, Rishika and the northern countries simultaneously. Thereafter, Arjuna crossed Dhavalgiri and reached the country of Kimapurush, protected by Dumputra, where the Kinnars(divine beings) lived. He conquered that country after a fierce battle and reinstated the king on the condition that he would continue to pay taxes. After that, he went to Hatak country and conquered it. Upon reaching Manasarovar,

Arjun also took control over the region protected by Gandharvas near Hatak Desh. Then, Arjun took Harivarsha under his control and obtained many gems from there. After this, Arjun went to Nishadha mountain and defeated its inhabitants. Thereafter, crossing the huge Nishadha mountain, he reached the divine Ilavritavarsha, which was the central part of Jambudweep. There, Arjun saw divine men who looked like Devtas and were as powerful as them. Arjuna conquered the inhabitants of that country in a war, imposed taxes on them and appointed those fortunate men as kings. Then, taking gifts of divine gems along with clothes and ornaments, Arjuna happily proceeded further north . After that, he went further north. He then, conquered the regions ruled by the Snake lords. Moving further west, Arjuna reached the Gandhamadana mountain and conquered its inhabitants.After crossing the Gandhamadana mountain, Arjuna reached Ketumalavarsha, endowed with gems and inhabited by devta-like men and women. After conquering that varsha, Arjuna made it a taxpayer and taking rare gems from there, he returned to the central Ilavrita. Thereafter,Arjun along with many warriors, went to the region protected by the Gandharvas and, along with the Gandharvas, took over that country. There, Arjun faced many enemies and defeated them. Then he went to the White Mountain and conquered its inhabitants there. After crossing it, Arjuna entered the Hiranyakavarsha. In Hiryanakavarsha, the beautiful inhabitants welcomed him with many jewels and gems.

As he ventured further, he was stopped by huge gate guards who joyfully said:. "Parth! You cannot conquer this city in any way. Auspicious Arjun! Return from here. Achyuta! You have come this far, and that is enough. The person who enters this city surely dies. Brave! We are very pleased with you. Reaching here itself is your great victory, Arjun! Nothing worth conquering is visible here. This is Uttar Kurudesh. War does not take place here. Kuntikumar! Even if you enter this place, you will not be able to see anything here because nothing here can be seen with the human body. O jewel of the Bharat clan, Purushsingh! If you want to do some other work here apart from fighting, then tell us. At your behest, we will do that work ourselves. " Then Arjun happily replied that he only sought tribute for the king. The gatekeepers then gave Arjun many divine clothes, divine ornaments, divine silken clothes and deerskin in the form of a deer. Thus, Arjun fought many battles with the Kshatriya kings and robbers and conquered the northern direction. After subduing the kings, he took taxes and reinstated them. Arjun, taking with him wealth and various kinds of gems and all the horses like Tittiri, Kalmash, Sugga and Peacock, which were as fast as the wind and surrounded by the four-fold army, returned to his glorious Indraprastha.

At the same time, Bhimsen went to conquer the East. First, he conquered Gondak and Mithila Kingdom. After that, he moved further and defeated King Sudharma of Dashan. Then he defeated King Rochman of Ashva

Kingdom. Afterwards, he turned southwest, where he conquered the great city of Pulinda and made King Sumitra submit to him. Then he went to the Chedi Kingdom, where Shishupal happily surrendered . Next, Bhīmasena,having subdued his enemies, defeated the king of Kumaradeśa, Śreṇimān, and the king of Kosala, Bṛhadbala. After this, Bhimsen, subdued the righteous king of Ayodhya, Mahabali Dirgha Yagna, with gentle diplomacy. Thereafter, Bhimsen conquered Gopalakaksha and the northern Kosala , bringing Parthiva, the ruler of Malla Rashtra, under his control. Then he marched to the Himalayas and swiftly took control of the entire Jalodbhava . Bhimasena displayed immense bravery and defeated the King of Kashi, Subahu, who never turned his back in battle. Afterwards,he defeated Rajarajeshwara Kratha near Suparsva, who bravely faced him in battle. Then, Bhimsen conquered the countries of Matsya, Mahabalo Malad, Anagh and Abhaya and also conquered Pashubhumi (the place near Pashupatinath - Nepal). On his return from there, he overcame the Madadhar mountain and subdued inhabitants of Somdheya. After that, he marched northward and took control of Vatsabhumi. He then successively defeated several rulers like the lord of the Bhargas, the lord of the Nishadas and Maniman. After this, Bhīmasena quickly subdued the southern Malla region and the Bhogavan mountain with little resistance. He persuaded the Sharmakas and Varmakas to surrender peacefully. King Janaka of Videha was also defeated by Bhimsen without any aggressive effort. He then subdued Shakas and the Barbarians through deceit.While staying in Videha, Bhima defeated the seven Kirata kings living near the Indra mountain. After that Bhimsen defeated the kings of the Suhya and Prasuhya countries, who had large armies and proceeded toward the Magadh country. On the way, he defeated Danda-Dandadhar and other kings and with them reached the city of Girivraja. There, he consoled Sahadeva and reinstated him as a king under the condition of paying tribute.With them, Bhimsen then attacked Karṇa(suryaputra). Bhimsen waged war against Karṇa, with a four division army,that shook earth. After defeating and subduing Karṇa, Bhima conquered the mountain kings.Then, Bhīmasena killed the most powerful king of Modagiri in fierce battle with his own strenght. Later , he fought with the mighty king Paundrak Vasudeva, the ruler of Paundrak country, who lived in the basin of the river Kosin river and was highly reowned. Both were fierce warrior ,but Bhimsen defeated Paundrak Vasudeva, and advanced to the Vanga Kingdom. There, Bhimasena, defeated Samudrasena, Bhupala Chandrasena, King Tamralipta, the king of Karvata and the king of Suhma and subdued all the Mlecchas living along the coast. After collecting vast wealth and precious gems from them, he moved to Lohitya Country. There, he conquered many mlechha kings living on the sea islands and acquired various gems from them in exchange for wealth.Finally , Bhimsena returned to Indraprastha and handed over all the wealth to Dharmaraja Yudhisthir. Meanwhile,

Nakula conquered the south with the help of Ghatochkach, and Sahadev conquered the west.

After that, they went to Indraprastha and gave all the jewels, money, elephants and the other riches they had collected as tax to king Yudhisthir. This was how Pandavs completed the "Digvijay Yatra". After the success of Digvijay Yatra, King Yudhisthir, on the advice of Shree Krishna, decided to perform the Rajsurya Yagya and invited all kings from across the world. On the day of Yagya, King Yudhisthir organized a huge sabha bhavan where all the kings and Sage sat in their respective places. There King Yudhisthra asked Bhishma whom he should worship first among the kings and sages, Bhishma replied, "Kunti's son! Shri Krishna is shining among all these kings with His brilliance, strength and valour, just like the Sun, the sun-light of the world, among the stars and planets. Just as a dark place becomes illuminated with the light of the rising sun and an airless place becomes alive with the circulation of air, in the same way our assembly is being delighted and illuminated by Shri Krishna (therefore, He is worthy of worship first). " Except for Shishupal, everyone agreed with him. This made Shishupal furious. He began abusing Shree Krishna and the Pandavas. He insulted Shri Krishna 99 times, and on the 100th times, he spoke derogatory words about Rukmini, the wife of Shri Krishna. This engraged Vasudev , and he beheaded Shishupal with his chakra. After killing him, Shri Krishna made Shishupal's sonthe king of the Chedi kingdom.

Thereafter, the Rajsurya yagya began with divine grace increasing the happiness of the King. Finally, with all the rituals and mantras completed, the yagya ended successfully. After that, King Yudhishthir gave generous dakshina to all the worthy brahmins and sages. He also gave gifts, who then returned to their respective kingdoms. The next day, after the Yagya ended, Ved Vyas came to King Yudhishthir 's court and told him about Shree Hari's prophecy regarding the mass killing of kshatriyas in the future war. This made the king anxious, and he took an oath that

"I will never speak bitter words to my brothers or other kings. I will happily obey my relatives and remain busy fulfilling their needs. By treating everyone equally, I will not discriminate between my children and others, as discrimination is the root cause of conflict in the world. By avoiding enmity and conflict and being dear to all, I will not be condemned."

The rest of the Pandavas welcomed his decision and followed his way. On the other hand, Duryodhan, on his way home, was consumed by various thoughts. He was alone ,brooding over the divine assembly of Dharmaraj Yudhishthira and the incomparable wealth and power he had witnessed. At that time, Duryodhan, seemed maddened. He did not respond to Shakuni who asked him repeatedly. Seeing his distress, Shakuni asked-"Duryodhan! From where did you get this sorrow, due to which you keep taking long sighs?" Then Duryodhana replied "Uncle! I have seen that this entire earth, won by the might of the weapons of the great white-vehicled Arjun, has come under the control of Yudhishthira. The Rajasuya Yagya of the mighty Yudhishthira has been completed in the same way as the Yagya of Devraj Indra among the gods. Seeing all this, I am filled with jealousy day and night, just like a small tap dries up quickly in the summer season. Also, see that Shri Krishna killed Shishupal, but no brave man was ready to take revenge for him. Just as the tax-paying merchants and Vaishyas would present themselves to the king with gifts of various kinds of gems, similarly, all the kings had presented themselves to King Yudhishthira with various kinds of precious gems. I am burning with jealousy on seeing that beautiful goddess Lakshmi present near Yudhishthira, son of Pandu, although my plight is not justified. " Burning with worry, Duryodhan continued "I will either enter the fire, consume poison or drown myself in water; I will not be able to survive anymore. Who will be such a powerful man in the world who will silently endure the increase of enemies and his poor condition? At this moment, I am neither a woman nor am I equipped with weapons, nor am I a man nor am I impotent, yet, despite seeing such great wealth that has come to the enemies, I am quietly enduring it. I am alone, not capable of grabbing that royal goddess Lakshmi, and I do not see any capable helper near me; that is why I am contemplating death. I had earlier tried to destroy Dharmaraja Yudhishthira, but after overcoming all those troubles, he continued to grow like a lotus in water. " Seeing his miserable condition

Shakuni consoled him and said "Duryodhan! You should not be jealous of Yudhishthira because the Pandavas have always enjoyed their fortune. You adopted many methods to bring them under your control, but you could not bring them under your control. O King, destroyer of enemies! You repeatedly plotted against the Pandavas, but those best of men managed to escape from all these troubles on their own. All the devatas, demons and humans combined cannot defeat Shri Krishna. It is because of his brilliance that King Yudhishthira has prospered; what is there to mourn over? The Pandavas, having deviated from their objective, have acquired their ancestral kingdom by continuous efforts and that ancestral property has increased a lot today due to their brilliance, so what is the need to do for it? Arjuna has satisfied Agnidev and obtained the Gandiva bow, the infinte quiver and many divine weapons. With that excellent bow and the strength of his arms, he has subdued all the kings, so what is the need to mourn for this? The great archer and mighty Dronacharya is ready to help you, along with his son, Ashwatthama. Radhanandan Sutaputra Karṇa, Maharathi Kripacharya, I along with my brothers and King Bhurishrava - you too conquer the whole earth with all of them" Then Duryodhan asked Shakuni about attacking the Pandavs. Shakuni replied that he had a better way to defeat pandavs without bloodshed. When Duryodhan asked about it. Then, Shakuni replied "King!Kunti's son Yudhishthira loves gambling very much, but he does not know how to play it. If Maharaja

Yudhishthira is called to gamble, he will not be able to back out. I am very skilled in gambling. There is no one else on earth who can match me in this art. Not just here, there is no one like me in the three worlds who knows the art of gambling. Therefore, son of Kuru! You call Yudhishthira for gambling. I am skilled in throwing dice. I will certainly get Yudhishthira's kingdom and the illustrious royal wealth, there is no doubt about it. Now you must tell this to your father and make him convinced to invite Yudhishthira for Gambling." After reaching Hastinapur, the first thing they did was to go to the King Dritharasthra to execute their plan of dethroning Yudhisthir.First, Duryodhan tried to convince king by expressing his insecurities about Pandav. Then shakuni joined him, boasting about his dice skill and how he could easily takeaway Yudhishthir wealth and power . Even then, the king remained hesitant. So Duryodhan reminded him of Arjun and Bhimsen's power and warned that if nothing was done, they would soon take over Hastinapur. He even said that not even Bhishma, Drona, Kripa, or Karna would be able to stop them. As a final move, Duryodhan threatened to commit suicide if the king refused to act. This deeply worried King Dhritarashtra. Knowing his son's intentions, he finally agreed to organize a gambling match between Yudhishthir and Duryodhan. After this, he called Mahatma Vidur and instructed him to prepare a special committee for gambling and to go to Indraprastha to invite Yudhishthir for the game of dice.

GAMBLING

When King Dhritarashtra forcefully sent him, Vidurji rode on a chariot drawn by very swift, powerful and well-controlled horses and went to the Indraprastha, to the palace of Yudhishthira. There he conveyed the king's message to Yudhishthir and warned him about the bad intentions of kauravs and Shakuni skills. But King Yudhisthir, remembering his oath, agreed to go to Hastnapur along with his family to play the game of dice. Then vidur returned to Hastinapur and informed king Drithrasthra about Yudhisthir's agreement to play the game of dice. Then, Yudhishthira, reached Hastinapur at the time set by Dhritarashtra and met Him in his Palace. Similarly, Yudhishthira met Bhishma, Drona, Kripacharya and Ashwatthama according to their senority and respect. Thereafter, Yudhishthira met Somadatta,Duryodhan, Shalya, Shakuni and the kings who had already arrived there. Then, after meeting Dushasan, all his brothers, King Jayadrath and all the Kauravas, Yudhishthira, along with his brothers, entered the palace of Dhritarashtra and saw the devoted Gandhari Devi sitting with her daughters-in-law. Yudhishthira bowed to Gandhari, and Gandhari also blessed them kindly. Then he met king Dhritarashtra, again and took his blessing. After that, Yudhisthir, along with other Pandavs, went to their respective room. After spending the night comfortably, he performed his daily chores such as morning and evening prayers, and then went to the gambling hall. There, the gamblers welcomed him. Yudhishthira and other Pandavs entered assembly and met all the kings. After honoring the revered kings one by one according to their age and position, they sat on unique seats covered with beautiful carpets . After everyone get settled Shakuni said to Yudhishthira "Maharaj Yudhishthira! The dice-throwing cloth has been laid out in the assembly; everyone is waiting for you. Now, you should get a chance to gamble by throwing the dice". Then Yudhishthira asked, "Gambling is a type of deceit and is the cause of sin! Neither can Kshatriya-like valour be displayed in it, nor is there any definite policy for it. Then why do you praise gambling?" Then Shakuni Replied" "One who understands in advance the number on which the dice will fall, who knows how to counter the cheaters, who remains actively involved in all activities of the game, and who is extremely intelligent and aware of all aspects of gambling—he is the real player. Such a player tolerates the dishonest attempts of others. " After hearing Shakuni's words , Yudhishthir against repeated that gambling is a sin and would lead to hatred and destruction.Interrupting him, Shakuni said " "Yudhishthira, when a learned scholar goes to another scholar to win them over, he uses only politeness. A scholar defeats the ignorant with strategy, yet people do not call this deceit. Dharma-raja! One who is skilled in the art of gambling wins over the unskilled through cleverness. Even a warrior skilled in weapons defeats the weak by cunning. Thus, in all walks of life, the learned overcome the ignorant through clever means—but this is not called cunning by the people. If you feel you will be treated unfairly and know the truth of this game, then walk away from . " Then Yudhishthira Replied, "O King! I never step back if called upon; this is my fixed vow. Destiny is powerful, and I am under its control." After this conversation between Yudhisthir and Shakuni, the game of dice begans with everyone's consent. Yudhisthir 1ˢᵗ staked his precious unique jewels , which he lost due to Shakuni's mastery in the game of dices. In this way, he lost all the wealth he had gained from other kings. Seeing this deceitful game , Vidur angrily warned Drithrasthra about the consequences of Gambling and the malicious intentions of Karṇa and Duryodhan. This made Duryodhan angry. he replied to Vidur, "Vidura, you always boast of your fame at the cost of our dignity and constantly criticise us—the sons of Dhritarashtra. We know whom you favour, yet you always insult us, considering us fools. We have earned great wealth by defeating our enemies. Vidura! Do not speak harshly here. You were pleased making peace with our enemies, and even after we accepted peace, you keep praising them. A man who speaks harshly becomes an enemy. Even when people praise their enemies, they hide their real feelings. Shameless Vidura! Why don't you stay silent and follow the same code of morality? Why do you obstruct our work? You keep babbling anything that comes to your mind. A person biased towards the enemy should not be kept in the house. So go wherever you wish. No matter how much you try to console a promiscuous woman with sweet words, she still leaves her husband" Vidur again tried to convince Dhritarashtra and Duryodhan, but both ignored him and continue with the game.One by one, as King Yudhishthir lost all his wealth, he staked his entire kingdom and lost that too .Still hopeful, he gambled his younger Brother Nakul, hoping to win back his kingdom , but loses him as well. After that, he staked Sahadev and lost him too. This is how he lost everything- his wealth, kingdom, brother and even himself. Shakuni, adept in the art of dice, informed King Yudhishthira about his loses and then announced to the renowned kings seated in the assembly about the defeat of the Pandavas. After that Shakuni said-"O King! Your beloved Draupadi is a gamble which you have not lost till now; hence you should gamble with Panchal princess Krishna and win yourself back through her." Yudhisthir, seeing no choice and bound by his oath, staked his wife Draupadi in the game. But due to misfortune and Shakuni's mastery in the dice, he lost her too.This dreadful moment—Yudhishthira losing Draupadi—intensified the tension in the sabha. Mahatma Vidura placed his hand on his head and fainted. Meanwhile, Bharika, Somadatta (Pratipa's grandson), Bhishma, Sanjaya, Ashwatthama, Bhurishrava, and Yuyutsu—all bowed their heads like defeated snakes, sighed deeply, and rubbed their hands in despair.On the other hand, Dhritarashtra became so overjoyed that he could not hide it and exclaimed,"Is our side winning?" Karṇa, along with the other Kauravas, felt extreme joy, while the rest of the sabha was grief-stricken, and tears flowed from their eyes.

Thereafter, Duryodhana ordered Vidura to bring Draupadi to the court. Then, Vidur, with red eyes, curses Duryodhan and says, "This Duryodhan will destroy the Kuru clan. A very terrible destruction will come about through him. He does not even listen to the scholarly advice of his friends; his greed is increasing. Soon the whole Kuru dynasty will end through him".

Thus, while insulting Vidur, Duryodhan ordered Pratilomi to bring Draupadi to the court. Then, Pratilomi went to Draupadi's room and said,"Daughter of Drupada, Dharmaraja Yudhishthira had gone mad from gambling. He lost everything and even put you at stake. Then, Duryodhana won you. Now, you must come to Dhritarashtra's palace. I am taking you there to make you work as a maid." Then Draupadi replied "Pratilomi! How can you say such a thing? Which prince will gamble by putting his wife at stake? Has King Yudhishthira gone so mad in the intoxication of gambling that he has no more money left to offer?Then you must go and ask King Yudhisthir, whom he did lost first himself or me." Then Pratilomi returned to the court and conveyed Draupadi's message to both Duryodhan and Yudhisthir. Yudhisthir remained silent, but Duryodhan again ordered him to bring her to the court by asking, "Ask your question in the court in front of everyone to your respectable husbands". Then Pratilomi did as instructed, but Draupadi still refused to come to the court. Instead she said "So that my Dharma (righteousness) is not violated, go to the elders of the kuru assembly and ask them this Dharma-related question on my behalf: 'What should I do at this time?' Whatever these righteous, wise and great men command me to do, I will surely do that. " Hearing this , Suta Pratilomi returned to the assembly and repeated Draupadi's words. But due to Duryodhan's obstinacy, everyone in the court sat with their faces downcast; no one uttered a word. Pratilomi, under the Duryodhana's control and fearing the anger of Draupadi, disregarded his own honor and again asked the councilors - "What answer should I give to Draupadi?" Then, Duryodhana ordered Dushasan to bring Draupadi to the court. Hearing his brother's order, Dushasan stood up with eyes blazing red and stormed into the Pandav's palace.He said this to Draupadi. "Panchali! Come! You were won in gambling. Krishna! Leave your shyness now and look at Duryodhana. Lotus-eyed Draupadi! We have won you lawfully. Now serve the Kauravas. Come to the royal court". Then, Dushasan roaring with anger, grabbed her long blue, flowing hair and forcibily dragged her, disregarding the bravery of the Pandavas. Draupadi, distressed and helpless, cried out like an orphan . Just like the wind bends the banana tree, in the same way, he forcefully pulled Draupadi . Her body bent as he dragged her. She said softly, "Oh, foolish and evil Dushasan, I am menstruating, and I have only one piece of garment on my body. It is improper to bring me to court in this condition". Ignoring her plea, Dushasan tightrened his grip and shouted, "Draupadi! Whether you are menstruating, wearing only one garment or naked, we have won you in gambling; hence, you have become our dasi. You must live among the maids as we command." At that moment, Draupadi's hair was dishevelled and half of her garment had slipped off due to Dushasan violence. She felt deeply ashamed and burned with inner fury. In that condition, she softly spoke as follows. "You are dragging a menstruating woman into this assembly of warriors. This is a sinful act. No one here is condemning your evil. Surely, they are all under your influence. Shame! The Dharma of the kings of the Bharata dynasty has perished, and even those who know Kshatriya Dharma remain silent!". Turning to the elders, she asked," O! Great men, whom did Yudhisthir lose first, me or himself?? please answer me". Seeing her in such a dreadful state, Karṇa and Dussashan began to laugh,and mockingly called her dasi. This embarrased Vikrana, Duryodhan's brother.Like Draupadi, he also questioned the Kuru's elders and urged them to answer her question. This made Karṇa angry, and he rebuked ViKarṇa, saying, "Vikarna, in this world, many things yield opposite results. Just like fire can burn itself, some people destroy the family into which they are born. A disease grows within the body but weakens it. Animals graze on grass yet trample it underfoot. Similarly, though you were born into the Kurukula, you now threaten to harm it. Vikarna! Drona, Bhishma, Kripa, Ashwatthama, the wise Vidura, Dhritarashtra, and Gandhari—they all possess greater wisdom than you.

O younger brother of Duryodhana! You do not understand true Dharma. You say Draupadi, though won, was not truly won? You sound like a fool. O son of Dhritarashtra! How can you claim Draupadi was not won? Didn't Yudhishthira, the eldest of the Pandavas, stake everything in the gambling hall?". Then he turned toward Draupadi and, seeing her with lustful eyes, he said.

एको भर्ता स्त्रिया देवैर्विहितः कुरुनन्दन । एका
त्वनेकवशगा बन्धकीति विनिश्चिता ॥ ३५॥
अस्याः सभामानयनं न चित्रमिति मे मतिः । एकाम्बरधरत्वं
वाप्यथ वापि विवस्त्रता ॥

O son of Kuru! The gods have ordained a woman to have only one husband, but this Draupadi is under the control of many husbands, so she is a prostitute. Her being brought to the court is not unusual. She can be brought here even if she is wearing only one garment or naked, this is my clear opinion.

(Sabhaparva, Dyutaparva, chap 68, shlok 35 & 36)

After expressing his opinion in the kurusabha, Karna ordered Dusashan to disrobe Draupadi and Pandav. Listening to Karṇa's words, the pandavs immediately throw their clothes on the ground. Then, Dushasan forcibly grabbed Draupadi's clothes and began pulling them in the assembly. As her clothes were being pulled, Draupadi began praying to Shree Krishna. She repeatedly called out the names of 'Govind' and

'Krishna' and silently meditated upon Shree Krishna, the incarnation of Bhagwan Narayana, the great grandfather of the universe, who gave protection in times of crisis. "O Govinda! O Dwarkadheesh Shri Krishna, the beloved of the cowherds, Keshav! The Kauravas are insulting me. Do you not know? O Nath! O Ramanath! O Vijnanam! O trouble-destroyer Janardan! I am drowning in the sea of the Kauravas; please save me!" Shri Krishna, in the form of Sachchidananda Mahayogin, the Universal Spirit, entered her clothes in the form of air and covered Draupadi with various beautiful garments. As her clothes were being pulled, countless similar clothes began to appear. Due to the power of Dharma, hundreds of colorful garments kept manifesting. At that moment, the great uproar broke out. Seeing the miraculous event , all the kings started praising Draupadi and criticizing Dushasan.Among them , Bhimsena rubbed his hands on his chest, cursed (made a vow) , his lips quivering with anger and with a terrible roar, took a dreadful vow: "O kings! This unrighteous misrule is a disgrace to the Bharata dynasty. I will tear open the chest of this sinner in battle and drink his blood. If I do not fulfill this vow, may I not attain the sacred path of my ancestors! ". Upon hearing this terrifying and hair-raising oath, all the kings condemned Dushasan and praised Bhimasena . When a pile of clothes gathered in the court, Dushasan felt ashamed and sat down quietly. Then Vidur calmed the court and asked the same question to the Elders and Yudhisthir. "Whom did Yudhisthir lose first himself or

Draupadi?" But still, no one answered him. Then, Duryodhan rose and insulting Vidur, he said,"Panchali! These people should tell these great kings that Yudhishthira had no right to put them at stake. All the Pandavas together should prove Dharmaraja Yudhishthira a liar. Then Panchali! You will be freed from the bondage of being dassi. This son of Dharma, Mahatma Yudhishthira, is as radiant as Indra and is always established in Dharma. Did he have the right to put you at risk or not? Let him tell you himself; then, as per his words, you should soon take refuge in either being Dassi or get free from this bond. Draupadi! All these noble-natured Kuru clansmen in this assembly are sad only for you, and seeing your unfortunate husbands, they are unable to give the right answer to your questions. "On one side, members of the court praised Duryodhana and roared while shaking their garments; on the other hand, there was chaos and crying. Hearing those words the Kauravas felt delighted. All the other kings respected Duryodhana, and called him the most righteous among the Kauravas. Then they all turned their faces towards Yudhishthira , hoping to hear what what the wise son of Pandu would say.They also waited to see how Arjuna,undefeated warrior would respond What would Bhimsen, Nakul and Sahadeva say? Those kings were very eager to hear them. When the noise subsided, Bhimsen raised his divine arm with sandalwood and said, "If this great Dharmaraja Yudhishthira were not like our father and the master of the Pandava lineage, we would not have tolerated the

Kauravas' cruelty. He is the lord of our virtue, penance, and even our lives. If he did not consider himself defeated before putting Draupadi at stake, then all of us are defeated because of his action. Had I not been defeated, then even a mortal man who merely touched Draupadi's hair would not have survived my wrath."
O kings! Look at my mighty arms, thick and round like a mace. Even Indra would not survive if he came between them. I am bound by Dharma. My elder brother's pride restrains me, and Arjuna also forbids me. That is why I am unable to act. But if Dharamraj permits me, then just as a lion seizes a deer, I shall crush these sinful sons of Dhritarashtra with the soles of my hands—without a sword!" Then the elders relaxes him saying, "You can do anything" Hearing Bhimsen's words, Karṇa becomes angry and said, ""O dear Draupadi! A slave, a son, and a woman—these three never own wealth. The wife of a poor daas, whose husband is a slave, and all the wealth of that daas belong only to his master. Princess! You must now go to King Duryodhana's house and serve everyone. This is your only duty now. From today, the sons of Dhritarashtra are your masters, not the sons of Kunti. Beautiful lady! Choose another husband now, so you may not have to become a slave again due to gambling. It is not shameful for a woman like you to act according to her husband's will. The whims of a woman in slavery are already known. You must now accept this dasya bhava." Then, Bhimsen didn't say anything to Karṇa, but instead, he blamed Yudhisthir for staking Draupadi , which led to all these terrible events and

became silent. Then, Duryodhan again asked Yudhisthir to answer Draupadi's question. Intoxicated with power and encouraged by Karṇa, Duryodhana insulted Bhimasena with gestures, removed the cloth from his thigh, and, smiling at Draupadi, showed her his left thighSeeing this, Bhimasena's eyes turned red with fury. He glared widely and shouted in front of the kings:. Duryodhana! If I do not smash this thigh of yours with my mace in the great war, then I, Bhimasena, do not deserve to attain the virtuous realms of my ancestors!" At that time, Bhimasena was filled with rage, and sparks of fire seemed to burst from his every pore—just as flames shoot out from a burning tree. Listening to this fierce oath of Bhimsen, Vidur warned Drithrasthra and Kaurav that Bhimsen's fury would burn them to the ground. But Duryodhan ignored him and again mocked Pandavs by repeating the same question.

Then Arjun said - "Kunti's son, the great Dharmaraja Yudhishthira, indeed had the right to stake us. But when he lost himself, then whose master was he? The Kauravas should ponder this.". Suddenly, a jackal entered King Dhritarashtra's fire chamber and howled loudly. Hearing the sound, donkeys brayed, and vultures and other fierce birds made ominous cries all around. Vidur and Gandhari also heard those dreadful sounds. That inauspicious signs were also perceived by Bhishma, Drona and Kripacharya. Then, Gandhari and Vidur, both deeply troubled, approached King Dhritarashtra with grief.Drithrasthra then said "O foolish Duryodhana! You are already defeated, even though you think you have won. You are ill-mannered! You speak sinfully to a woman of your clan—especially the wife of the Pandavas—in front of the noble Kuru elders." After saying this , King Dhritarashtra,with concern of his family's welfare, consoled Panchala princess Draupadi with wise words - "Daughter-in-law Draupadi! You are the best and most virtuous among my daughters-in-law. Ask me for a boon according to your wish. " She replied, "If you grant me a boon, I ask that King Yudhishthira, who follows all the Dharma, should be freed from the feeling of being a dass. So that other princes may not call my intelligent son Prativindhya a 'son of a das' due to ignorance. "

Then Drithrasthra asked for Second Boon.

In reply, Draupadi asked to free herself and the rest of the Pandavas from the Das Bhav with their weapons and become independent. Then King Drithrasthra accepted her wish and freed them from their Dassatva. To save his sons from Bhimsen's fury, he returned Pandav their wealth and honorably sent them to their Kingdom. Knowing that King Dhritarashtra had ordered the Pandavas to leave, Dushasan immediately went to his brother Duryodhan, who was sitting with his ministers (Karṇa and Shakuni) and spoke in grief as follows: "Maharathi! You must know that the wealth which we had acquired with great difficulty is being destroyed by our old father. He has handed over all the wealth to the enemies." Hearing this, Duryodhana, Karṇa and Shakuni, began consulting each other to take revenge on the Pandavas. Then all three of them warned Drithrasthra about the archery skills of Arjun and how he had defeated devtas along with Devraj Indra, and even Bhishma, Dronacharya, Ashwathamma, and Kripacharya wouldn't stand a chance against Arjun. This made King Drithrasthra insecure and worried, so he sent his messenger to Pandavs, who were on their way to Indraprastha with an invitation to another game of dice. Thus, on receiving this invitation, King Yudhisthir accepted it, remembering his oath despite knowing what happened in the previous game. This saddened Pandav greatly, but they followed in their brother's footsteps. The Pandavas again entered that assembly. Seeing them, their friends felt great pain in their hearts.Pandavs, subjugated by destiny, went there and sat quietly to start the game of gambling again for the destruction of the entire world. Then Shakun said, "You have done very well to return for the game of dice. Now, only one bet will be placed for gambling, listen to it—if you defeat us in gambling, we will wear deerskin and enter the great forest. We will stay there for twelve years and complete the thirteenth year by remaining unknown to the people in the crowd. If we come to the notice of the people in the thirteenth year, then we will again stay in the forest for twelve years. If we win, then you will live in the forest with Draupadi wearing deerskin for twelve years and one year in disguise." Despite everyone being against the game of dice,

Yudhishthira, bound by destiny, played the game and lost just like in the previous game. This saddened Pandavs very much, and they started preparing for their exile to the forest. But on the other hand, Karna and Duryodhana became very happy. They had the upper hand and, due to their ego, started humiliating the Pandavas. This made Bhimsen extremely furious, and he took an oath that after the thirteenth year, in the war, he would kill all the Kauravas, Arjun would kill Karna, and Sahadev would kill Shakuni. Thus, the Pandavas, along with Draupadi, left the palace in deerskin and moved toward the forest, leaving Mother Kunti in Vidura's house. While they were passing the boundary of Hastinapur, people of every varna, from Brahmin to Shudra, saw them. Seeing them in such a condition, their eyes filled with tears, and they started cursing Dhritarashtra and his sons along with Karna.

Note: Karna had always played a major role in every conspiracy against the Pandavas. From the entire gambling incident, we can conclude that Karna was not a good man but an extremely evil one who viewed women as property. He was the one who ordered Dushasana to disrobe Draupadi and even instructed him to take her to his room.

VAN VAS

After losing the game, Pandavs went to the forest named Kamyavan. Meanwhile, in the inner chambers of the King's palace, Vidur exhorted King Drithrasthra to free Pandav from their exile and return their Kingdom. When Duryodhan came know about this, he decided to kill himself. However, Shakuni explained to him that Pandav would never broke their vow of exile. Dussashan also agreed with him but this still did not satify Duryodhan. Then Karṇa ferrociousley said, "We all are servants and arms of King Duryodhan; hence, we all will together do his favourite work, but we are unable to leave laziness and engage in his favourite activities. 'My opinion is that we should wear armour, mount our chariots, take up arms and attack the exiled Pandavas together to kill them . When all of them die and become peaceful and reach an unknown destination, i.e. the other world, then the sons of Dhritarashtra and all of us will be free from all the quarrels. My opinion is that as long as they are in trouble, as long as they are immersed in glory and as long as they are free from friends and helpers, they can win the war. " Having thus conversed among themselves, filled with anger and enthusiasm, they all sat on separate chariots, determined to kill the Pandavas and left the city together. Seeing them go towards the forest, through his Divine eyes, Maharishi Ved Vyas appeared there suddenly and stopped them. Then he directly went to

King Drithrasthra and warned him to stop Duryodhan from going after the exiled Pandavs. He declared that if Duryodhan did so, he and his friend(Karṇa) would be killed by Pandavas. In Kamya forest, Shree Krishna came to meet Pandav .He told them that due to war between him and Demon King Shalvya, he could not come to Hastinapur on the day of the Gambling match . Had he been there, then this terrible event would never take place and who humiliated and assaulted Draupadi would already be dead at his hand. Then he advised Arjun to worship Bhagwan Rudra, saying that only Rudra dev's grace would he able to defeat Dronacharya and Bhishma in the battle that would take place in the fourteenth year of their exile. Then Arjun took everyone's blessing and went toward Mount Indrakeel to worship Bhagwan Rudra. Then, the rest of the Pandavs, along with sages and with the blessing of Shree Krishna, began their Tirth Yatra. On Mount Indrakeel, Arjun performed tremendous penance which attracted Rudra dev's . Then Bhagwan Shiva decided to test him and appeared in the form of a Hunter before Arjun. He challenged Arjun to a battle and absorbed all his weapons, including the Ghandiv bow. Seeing all his weapons gone, Arjun began wrestling with the Hunter(Mahadev).Pleased with Arjuna's strength and devotion, Mahadev revealed his true form . Arjun was overjoyed and began praising Bhagwan Shiva. Then Mahadev pulled him with both hand and hugged him. He consoled Arjun and told him that he (Arjun) and Shree Krishna were the reincarnation of Bhagwan Nar and Narayan, who had performed tremendous penance of him(Mahadev) and killed many mighty Daityas. He assured Arjuna that no one could defeat him neither in this world nor in next(swarga). After that, he returned Arjun's weapons and granted him Pashupatastra ,warning him never to use it weaker opponent.He also insricted him on using the cosmic weapon. Then, along with Mata Parvati, he left for the Himalayas. Thereafter, Indra, along with Yamraj, Varun and Kuber, came to honor Arjun on Indraneel Mountain and gave him Divine weapons. Indra then took Arjun to Swarga on his chariot, where all devta gave him their divine weapons and taught him how to use them .Then, he met Chitrasen, his old friend ,who taught him the art of divine music and dance. After mastering the use of divine weapons, Devraj requested Arjun to defeat the enemy of the Devtas :the Nivatkavach and Piloma Asuras. Arjun went alone to patal loka on Indra's chariot. He fought a fierce battle against three crore Nivatkavach, and killed them using divine weapons. While returning, he saw an island full of asuras . Matali, the charioteer, told him that these were Kalakeyas & pilom asuras , who were more powerful than Nivatkavach. Arjun then turned chariot toward that island and attacked the asuras , but his weapons did little damage . Remembering Bhagwan Rudra's word, he used Pashupatastra . Thereafter, a huge army of terrifying beasts emerged the astras and attacked the Asuras, killing them all in an instant before vanishing. After killing asuras, Arjun returned to swarga, where

Devraj welcomed him wholeheartedly and gifted him divine armor and clothes. Meanwhile, in the Himalayan region, during the Tirth yatra, Bhimsen met Hanuman while searching for lotus for Draupadi. Hanuman taught him the art of using strenght and wrestling. After meeting Hanuman, Bhimsen resumed his search of lotus and eventually found the lotus in the pond guarded by Kubera's guard and Krodhavash rakshas. Bhimsen killed them all and obtained the lotus from the river.He then returned to Pandav's dweling and gave the lotus to Draupadi.Sometime later, on Gandhmadhan Mountain, Arjun returned to the Pandavs, and narrated everything that had happened in swarga and how he defeated the mighty asuras.

GANDHRAVA WAR

After completing their Tirthyatra, Pandavas returned to the Dwaita forest to spend the rest of their exile near the Hastinapur. When Karṇa came to know about Pandavs staying nearby, he said to Duryodhan, "Maharaj! You should go there adorned with royal wealth. Just as the Sun torments the world with his brilliance, in the same way, torment the sons of Pandu. The happiness a man gets from seeing the plight of his enemies is greater than that of gaining wealth, sons, or even a kingdom. What greater joy could one who seeks fulfillment feel than seeing Arjuna in an ashram wearing valkala (bark garments) and mriga-chala (deerskin)? Let your queens wear beautiful saris and go to the forest wrapped in bark and deerskin. Let them witness the sorrowful Draupadi, who in turn should be saddened upon seeing them. The Pandavas, deprived of wealth, should curse their fate again and again. The humiliation they faced in the assembly would not pain them as much as seeing your prosperity now." Then, Duryodhan sadly said that his father would never allow him to go there. Karṇa smiled and said, "II will tell you the solution I have thought of. Listen, Nareshwar! All the places where cows dwell are in this Dwaita Van only, and you are always invited to visit them. So, we can go there under the pretext of inspecting those places.

It is always acceptable to travel for inspecting your cows. If you use this excuse, your father will surely allow you to go "`Thereafter, seeing their plan succeeding, all of them laughed and clapped each other's hands in joy. Then, having made their decision, they met King Dhritarashtra. Using Karṇa 's suggestion, they successfully convinced King Dhritarashtra to permit a journey to the Dwaita forest. After receiving the permission of Dhritarashtra, Duryodhan left the city along with Karṇa and a large army. King Duryodhan camped two miles away from the city. From there, he proceeded toward the Dwaita van and the sacred lake with all his vehicles.King Duryodhana, camping at different spots in the forest, reached the cow-sheds and set up his camp there. The people accompanying him also camped in the surrounding area, which was full of all qualities: beautiful, well-known, watered and had dense groves of trees. Separate camps were set up near Duryodhana's tent for his brothers Karna, Shakuni, Dushasana, and others. . Once the inspection was done, he wandered around happily, accompanied by cowherd. Duryodhana and his companions enjoyed milk and other dairy products, indulging in all kinds of pleasures. They admired the beauty of the forests and gardens, where intoxicated bumblebees hummed and the sweet cries of peacocks echoed all around. Gradually, they reached the most sacred lake, named Dwaita. Duryodhana then ordered his thousands of servants to prepare a playground there. When the army commander accompanying him reached near the lake, the Gandharvas stopped him at the forest entrance. Seeing the lake surrounded by the Gandharva army, Duryodhana's soldiers returned and informed him of the situation. Duryodhana became angry and sent a message through his commander to the Gandharvas, demanding that they vacate the lake immediately. This angered the Gandharva King Chitrasena, who then challenged Duryodhana to warHearing the command, the commander quickly ran back and conveyed the Gandharva king's message to Duryodhana. Then Duryodhana said, "Even If Indra also comes here and plays with all the gods, then he too is displeasing me. You all should punish all these sinners. " Hearing these words, the mighty Kauravas and their thousands of warriors girded up their loins, ready for battle.Then, roaring loudly in all ten directions, Duryodhana forcefully trampled the Gandharvas and entered the Dwaita forest. At that time, other Gandharvas tried to stop the Kaurava soldiers peacefully.Despite these efforts, the soldiers ignored their words and entered the sacred forest. When all the Kauravas, including King Duryodhana, refused to stop even after peaceful persuasion, the Gandharvas roaming in the sky informed their king, Chitrasena, of everything. Hearing this, Gandharvaraj Chitrasen became very angry. Targeting the Kauravas, he ordered all the Gandharvas, "Hey! Suppress these evil ones". On receiving the order from Chitrasen, all the Gandharvas ran towards the Kauravas with their weapons. Seeing the Gandharvas approaching rapidly with weapons in hand, all the

Kaurava soldiers began to flee in all directions before Duryodhana. Even after seeing all the sons of Dhritarashtra fleeing the battle, Karṇa did not turn his back. Seeing the vast army of Gandharvas approaching him, Karṇa halted their advance by showering heavy arrows on them. Due to the agility of his hands, Sutaputra Karṇa injured hundreds of Gandharvas by showering arrows named Lohek Kshurapra, Vishik, Bhall and Vatsadant. By cutting off the heads of the Gandhavas, Karṇa destroyed the entire army of Chitrasena in a moment. As Karṇa began attacking them, the Gandharvas started gathering in hundreds and thousands. With the arrival of Chitrasena's extremely swift soldiers, the entire land became filled with Gandharvas in an instant. Thereafter King Duryodhana, Subala's son Shakuni, Dushasan and other sons of Dhritarashtra who came there, all mounted on horses making terrifying sounds like Garuda andslaughtering the Gandharva army. They placed Karṇa in front and again charged at the Gandharvas with great speed. A huge group of chariots accompanied them.They protected Karṇa and showered arrows upon the Gandharvas while maneuvering their chariots in strange patterns.Eventually, the Gandharvas began to weaken after being struck by Kaurava arrows, and seeing their pain, the Kaurava warriors began to roared with pride. Witnessing the frightened Gandharvas, Chitrasena became furious. He leapt from his seat with a firm resolve to kill his enemies and started the war using an illusory weapon .   All the Kauravas were entranced by

Chitrasena's illusion. Those warriors, who had earlier dared to win, became frightened and fled the battle, troubled by the enormous Gandharva army.As all the Kaurava soldiers began to flee, Suryaputra Karṇa stood firm like a mountain. Duryodhana, Karṇa, and Shakuni, though badly injured, continued to fight. Seeing this, all the Gandharvas assembled and formed groups of hundreds and thousands to attack Karṇa and kill him. Those mighty warriors surrounded Karṇa from all sides, attacking him with swords, belts, spears, and maces. Some cut the yoke of his chariot, some cut the flag and dropped it. Some shattered the bow (Ishadananda). Some Gandharvas killed Karṇa's horses, while others caused the charioteer to fall. The number of Gandharvas was in the thousands. They broke Karṇa's chariot into pieces. Then, Karna jumped off his chariot with sword and shield in hand and sat on Vikarṇa's chariot, urging the horses forward to save his life. When the Gandharvas chased away Karṇa, Duryodhana saw his entire army flee as well. Still, Duryodhana remained standing on the battlefield. He did not retreat. Seeing the massive Gandharva army approaching him, Duryodhana rained heavy arrows on them. But the Gandharvas ignored the arrow shower. They surrounded Duryodhana's chariot from all sides, killed his horses, and destroyed the chariot. At that moment, Duryodhana fell to the ground. Chitrasena immediately went and captured him alive. The Gandharvas also captured Duḥśāsana and other brothers of Duryodhana who remained there, along with their wives.

After Duryodhana's defeat, his soldiers who had earlier fled took refuge with the Pandavas and informed Yudhishthira of everything.On learning that not only Duryodhana but also his wives were captured by Gandharvas, Yudhishthira sent the rest of the Pandavas to fight them. A fierce battle ensued between the Gandharvas and the Pandavas. Unlike the Kauravas, the Pandavas defeated the Gandharvas and freed Duryodhana along with his brothers and wives. Thereafter, Yudhishthira, along with his brothers, gently said to the freed Duryodhana: "Brother! Never dare to do this again, Kurunandan! Now you go home safely with all your brothers as per your wish. Do not harbour any animosity towards us. " After receiving Yudhishthira's permission, Duryodhana bowed before him and left for his city. At that time, his heart trembled like that of a patient who had lost consciousness. He felt immense shame for his actions. His mind was filled with grief. Thinking about his humiliation,he moved towards the city with his fourfold army. On the way, he stopped at a place with abundant grass and water. Duryodhana left his vehicles there and stayed in a beautiful and pleasant place of his liking. He also ordered the elephants, horses, chariots, and foot soldiers to remain at their designated places. Karṇa approached Duryodhana and said:-

"Gandharvanandan! It is a matter of great fortune that you are alive. Luckily, we met again. Fortunately, you overcame the Gandharvas, who can take any form they wish. I was defeated by them and fled before your eyes. I couldn't rally the scattered army. My entire body was wounded by arrows, and I was in great pain. That is why I had to flee. O Bharata! It is astonishing to me that you, who escaped from such an inhuman war, are here safe with your women, army, and vehicles."

When Karṇa said this, Duryodhana tearfully told him everything—how he had been captured with his wives and how Arjuna had saved him from the Gandharvas. Overwhelmed with guilt, Duryodhana decided to fast unto death and told Karṇa to make Duḥśāsana the King of Hastinapur. Saying this, he sat on the ground and began his fast.

 Note: Karṇa, whom the so-called serials claim to be the strongest, couldn't defeat the Gandharvas even though he had his divine armour. On the other hand, Arjuna defeated the Gandharvas without any divine armour..

SECRET

Thereafter, consoling King Duryodhana, who was sitting on a fast unto death out of resentment, Subala's son Shakuni said

यत्र हर्षस्त्वया कार्यःसत्कर्तव्याश्च पाण्डवाः। तत्र शोचसि राजेन्द्र विपरीतमिदं तव ॥७॥ प्रसीद मा त्यजात्मानं तुष्टश्च सुकृतं स्मर। प्रयच्छ राज्यं पार्थानां यशो धर्ममवाप्नुहि ॥८॥ क्रियामेतां समाज्ञाय कृतज्ञस्त्वं भविष्यसि । सौभ्रात्रं पाण्डवैः कृत्वा समवस्थाप्य चैव तान् ॥९॥

The Pandavas have honoured you, and yet you are grieving. Where you should have been celebrating and welcoming the Pandavas, you are mourning. This behaviour of yours is completely the opposite. Therefore, bring happiness to your mind. Do not give up your body. Remember the good behaviour of the Pandavas towards you, and being satisfied, return their kingdom to them. By doing this, you will become a part of fame and Dharma

(Van parv, Ghoshyatra parva , chap 251,shloka 7,8 & 9)

Then Karṇa, who did not agree with Shakuni on returning the kingdom but still supported him, said that it was the Pandavas' duty to save him because he was their king. On hearing the words of Karṇa and Shakuni, Hearing the words of all his friends, Duryodhana became angry and said to them,

- Hearing the words of all his friends, Duryodhana became angry and said to them, "I do not need Dharma, wealth, happiness, prosperity, governance, or enjoyment. You all should not disturb my decision. Go away from here. My mind is determined to fast till death. You all should go to the city and always respect the teachers there". Duryodhana's friends, ministers, brothers, and relatives tried hard to convince him, but no one could change his decision, and they all returned to their respective places. Knowing Duryodhana's determination, the fierce Danavas and Daityas of the underworld, who had been defeated by the gods in the past, thought in their minds, " if Duryodhana dies in this way, our side will be destroyed "Therefore, to bring him to them, the Danavas and Daityas summoned a Kritya from a Yagya. TThen, a female Kritya emerged from the Yagya. The Asuras ordered her to bring Duryodhana to them. Saying "As you wish," the Kritya immediately left and, within the blink of an eye, reached the place where King Duryodhana was. Then, taking the king along with her, she reached Rasatala within two seconds and informed the demons of his arrival. Seeing King Duryodhana being brought there, all the demons gathered at night. Their hearts were filled with happiness, and they bloomed with joy. They proudly told Duryodhana.

"O King Suyodhana, who bears the burden of the Bharat dynasty! You are always surrounded by brave warriors and great-minded men; then why have you dared to fast unto death? A man who commits suicide attains degradation and is condemned in the world, which spreads infamy. ' Rajan! This suicidal thought of yours is destructive of dharma, wealth and happiness, fame, glory and bravery and increases the joy of enemies, hence stop it. Listen to a secret. O Lord of men! Your form is divine, and your body is also built wonderfully. Please be patient after listening to this from us. In the past, we had obtained you by worshipping Lord Shiva through austerities. The front portion of your body, which is above the navel, is shaped like a group of thunderbolts. It cannot be pierced by any weapon. Anagha! Similarly, Goddess Parvati has made your body below the navel flowery, which captivates the hearts of women with its beauty. Oh Rajsingh! You are not a human being; you are a divine being. Bhagadatta and other very brave Kshatriyas are endowed with divine weapons and are very courageous. They can destroy your enemies. Therefore, you didn't need to mourn. You have no fear.

Many brave asuras have appeared on the earth as powerful Kshatriya warriors to help you. Many other demons will also enter the bodies of Bhishma, Dronacharya, Kripacharya, etc., possessed by them; they will abandon mercy and fight with your enemies. When demons are enraged, the souls of Bhishma, Drona, etc., will also be taken over by those demons. In that condition, while attacking without any affection in the war, they will not spare even their sons, brothers, ancestors, relatives, disciples, family members, children and old people. Those brave men like Bhishma and Dronacharya will be helplessly deluded by ignorance (due to the fury of the demons). Their minds will become impure, and leaving aside their affection, they will happily attack with weapons. The reason behind this is the predestined promise. And the great Narakasur who had conquered all the realms but later got defeated by Shree Krishna will go possessed Karṇa, and he (Narakasur) going to make him thousand times more powerful then he was now.

हतस्य नरकस्यात्मा कर्णमूर्तिमुपाश्रितः । तद् वैरं संस्मरन् वीर योत्स्यते केशवार्जुनौ

The soul of Narakasur, who was killed by Shri Krishna, has entered the body of Karṇa. Braveheart! Remembering that enmity, he (Narakasur) will fight with Shri Krishna and Arjun.

(Van parva,Ghosh yatra parva , chap 252 , shlok 20)

Therefore, O son of Kuru! Do not be sad. This does not suit you. If you are destroyed, our side will be destroyed. Now you should not think unnecessarily any way. See, the devtas have taken shelter of the Pandavas, but our destination is always you ". Saying this to Duryodhan, the daityas and danavs took him to their heart like a son, assured him and stabilized his mind. After that, speaking loving words, they ordered Duryodhana to go and said, "Now you go and conquer the enemies."

 After the demons departed, the same kritya again took Duryodhana to the same spot where he had earlier sat for fasting unto death. After Kritya left, King Duryodhan thought all these things had been a dream. After reflecting on the words spoken by the demons, the evil-minded Duryodhana resolved in his mind, "I will defeat the Pandavas in the war." Meanwhile, Karṇa, too, being possessed by the inner soul of Narakasura, started making a cruel resolution to kill Arjuna. Demons had taken over the minds of Bhishma, Drona, Kripacharya, etc. Therefore, they did not have the same affection for the Pandavas.King Duryodhana did not reveal to anyone the things the demons had told him, whom he had called to his place at night through Kritya. After the night ended, Karṇa came to Duryodhana and again motivated him to fight against the Pandavas. Then Karṇa, under the influence of Narakasura, took an oath to kill Arjuna in front of him. This made Duryodhana very happy, and he hugged Karṇa. RRemembering the words of the demons, the best among men, Duryodhana, decided to fight the Pandavas and ordered his four-fold army—consisting of chariots, elephants, horses, and infantry—to get ready to go to Hastinapur. That huge army started moving like the flow of the Ganges.

Karṇa and the gambling expert Shakuni, along with all the brothers like Dushasana, Bhurishrava, Somadatta, and Maharaja Bahlika—all these gems of the Kuru clan—followed King Duryodhana, riding on various types of chariots, elephants, and horses. In a short time, all of them entered their capital, Hastinapur. Upon reaching Hastinapur, Bhishma warned Duryodhana about the strength of the Pandavas and advised him to return their kingdom to them. Then Bhishma taunted Karṇa, calling him a coward. . Duryodhana laughed at his words and suddenly left the place with his brother. But after that, in secret, he met Karṇa and told him what Bhishma had said. This made Karṇa angry, and under Narakasura's influence, he took an oath: "I cannot tolerate what Bhishma said in front of you. O destroyer of enemies! O son of the Bharat clan! The way he praised the Pandavas and criticized you is intolerable to me. So, please permit me to go on a Digvijaya with my servants, army, and horsemen. I will conquer the entire earth, including mountains, forests, and jungles. The land that the four powerful Pandavas conquered together, I will conquer for you alone; there is no doubt about it. Bhishma, the scoundrel of the Kuru clan, who has a corrupt mind, should witness this feat of mine with his own eyes. Bhishma, who criticizes the worthy and praises the unworthy, should see my strength today and curse himself. Now, give me your command. Your victory is certain. I speak this truth with full commitment and swear by touching my weapon. "Hearing this from Karṇa, King Duryodhana said to him with great happiness, "Brave one! When you are confident that you can kill all the enemies, then you should set out for Digvijaya. May you be blessed. Give me the order to make the necessary arrangements." On hearing this from Duryodhana, Karṇa gave orders to make all the necessary preparations for the journey. Thereafter, Karṇa, having bathed in water mixed with auspicious substances, was honored and praised with the blessed words of the people of the second caste. He then departed under an auspicious constellation, on an auspicious date, and at an auspicious time. At that moment, he echoed across the entire Triloka, along with the roaming ghosts, with the roar of his chariot.

DIG VIJAY

Thereafter, the great archer Karṇa, along with his huge army, surrounded the beautiful city of King Drupada from all sides. Then, after a great battle, he subdued the brave Drupada and forced him to give gold, silver, various gems and taxes. In this way, after defeating Drupada, Karṇa subdued his follower kings and collected taxes from them, too. Thereafter, he went to the north and subdued the kings there. After defeating Bhagadatta, Radhanandan Karṇa climbed the great mountain, Himalaya, fighting with the enemies. From there, he went in all directions and subjugated all the kings and conquered all the rulers of the Himalayan region and took taxes from them. Then he conquered the kings of Nepal and then descending from the Himalayas he attacked towards the east. After including Anga, Vanga, Kalinga, Shundik, Mithila, Magadh and Karkkhand in his kingdom, Karṇa also conquered Avashir, Yodya and Ahikshatra countries. Thus, after conquering the eastern direction, he entered Valsabhumi. After conquering Vatsabhumi, Karṇa took control of all the countries - Kevala, Mrittikavati, Mohan, Pattan, Tripuri and Kosala and after collecting taxes from all, proceeded (towards the south). After reaching the south, Karṇa defeated many great warriors. Karṇa fought with Rukmi in the southern states. Rukmi fought a very fierce battle at first but later on surrendered to him. He defeated the King of Kerala, Raja Neel and

Venudariputra on the battlefield and defeated other kings in the southern direction. After this, the mighty Karṇa, son of a charioteer, went to Chedi country and defeated the son of Shishupal and also subjugated his sibling kings. Subsequently, by subduing the kings of the Avanti country through military strategy, he also conquered the western direction by joining forces with the Yadavas of the Vrishni dynasty. After this, he went to the west and defeated the Yavan and Barbarian kings who were residents of the western country and collected taxes from them. In this way, he conquered the entire earth of the east, west, north and south and defeated all the republics like Mlechha, Vanvasi, Parvatiya, Bhadra, Rohitak, Agreya Malav, etc. After this, Sutanandan Karṇa, who worked according to the policy, happily conquered the Shashak and Yavana kings, too. In this way, Karṇa, under the influence of Narakasura, conquered the communities, conquered the whole earth and returned to Hastinapura. King Duryodhana, along with his brother, father and relatives, welcomed Karṇa,honoured him with due respect. After that, Duryodhana became very happy and announced Karṇa's victory everywhere. Then, Duryodhan happily said, ""Brave one! May you be blessed. What I could not get from Bhishma, Drona, Kripacharya, and Bahik, I received from you. Mahabahu Karṇa! What is the use of saying more? You listen to me. O noble man! I was safe only because I had you as my helper. All those Pandavas or other great kings could not even be equal to one-sixteenth of you." After coming back to Hastinapur,

Karṇa advised Duryodhana to perform a great and divine yagya, the same as Yudhisthira. So, he consulted a Brahmin priest. With their consultation, he performed the Vaishnav Yagya, which was as divine as the Rajasuya Yagya performed by King Yudhisthira.

DEAL

On knowing that the divine armour and earrings of Surya Dev not only belonged to Karṇa but also to Narakasura, he realized that Narakasura could become a great threat in the upcoming war of Dharma. So, he decided to take away the armour from Karṇa to prevent Narakasura from using its full power and becoming invincible. But before he could execute his plan, Narakasura, in the form of a Brahmin, informed Karṇa about Indra's plan through a dream. Later, when he woke up, Surya Dev also warned him about Indra Later on, when he wake up Surya dev also warned him about Indra. On the same day, Indra came to Karṇa disguised as a Brahmin and asked him for something. Karṇa offered him jewels, gold, a cow, etc, but the Brahmin refused and asked him for his divine armour.Karṇa humbly refused his demand and asked him to request anything else, but the Brahmin remained firm in his words. Then Karṇa finally said, "Prabhu! I already knew that you were coming. But Devendra! It is not fair that I make you unsuccessful. Indradev! If I give you both my earrings and armor, then I will be killed by my enemies, and you will be laughed at in the world. Therefore (Karṇa said remembering Surya's command-) O Sakra! You can give me some compensation and take my earrings and best armor; otherwise, I cannot give them back. " Then Indra told him to wish for anything in exchange for the divine armour and earrings of Surya Dev. Karṇa replied

वर्मणा कुण्डलाभ्यां च शक्तिं मे देहि वासव। अमोघां शत्रुसंघानां घातिनीं पृतनामुखे ॥ २१

O Vāsava! Take away my armour and earrings, and in return, grant me that invincible weapon of yours which is capable of destroying the enemy forces at the forefront of the battlefield.

(Van Parva , KundalHaran Parva , chap 310 , shloka 21)

he wanted Indra's Amogha Shakti to kill the enemy whom he feared. Knowing his evil intention, Indra said that this weapon would kill only one powerful enemy and then return to him. Indra then said

कुण्डले मे प्रयच्छस्व वर्म चैव शरीरजम् । गृहाण कर्ण शक्तिं त्वमनेन समयेन च ॥

Karna! Give me your natural armour and both of your earrings, and in return, accept this weapon of mine. As per this condition, let us exchange these items between us.

(Van Parva , KundalHaran Parva , chap 310 , shloka 23)

Hearing this, Karṇa happily accepted the weapon and, in return, gave away his divine armour to Indra. Thus, when the Kauravas came to know that Karṇa had given away his armour, they became very sad, while on the other hand, the Pandavas felt happy.

Note: As they propagated in TV serials, Karṇa did not donate his armor to Indra Dev; it was actually a proper deal between them.

THE THIRTEENTH YEAR

 After the end of the 12th year of Pandav's exile their Agyatvaas (incognito period) began, during which they chose the Matsya kingdom to spend their final year. . . Yudhisthir disguised himself as a brahmin named Kank, who teaches King Virat the game of dice. Arjun became a transgender Brihannala due to the curse he got from Urvashi Apsara in Swarga for calling her mother. As Brihannala, Arjuna taught dance and music to King Virat's daughter.Bhimsen disguised himself as Vallabh, the royal cook.Draupadi became Sairandhri, serving the queen, the wife of King Virat. Nakula and Sahadeva became Granthika and Arishtanemi, caretakers of cows and horses. Thus, all of them settled down in the Matsya kingdom.Everything went peacefully until one day when Kichaka, the king's brother-in-law, saw Sairandhri (Draupadi). He became obsessed with her and proposed to her, but she refused. Upon being rejected, Kichaka became furious and assaulted Draupadi in front of everyone in the king's court. Due to Kichaka's power, nobody dared to speak against him— everyone watched silently,including Yudhishthira, who was disguised as Kanka. However, due to Surya Dev's blessing, Kichaka failed to do any harm to Draupadi. After the incident, Draupadi secretly met Bhima and tearfully narrated everything to him. Bhima's eyes turned red with rage, but calming himself, he instructed her to invite Kichaka that night. He would disguise himself as her and kill him. Draupadi did exactly as Bhima told her.Kichaka, delighted, went to the hall as Draupadi had instructed. There, he saw Bhima disguised as Draupadi sitting on a sofa with his back turned. When Kichaka placed his hand on Bhima's shoulder, thinking he was Draupadi, Bhima threw him to the ground and killed him. The next day, Kichaka's brothers (Upkichakas) discovered his body. Enraged, they dragged Draupadi along with Kichaka's body to the cremation ground, intending to burn her alive with their brother. When Bhima heard about this, he ran like a tornado toward the cremation ground, destroying everything in his path. Upon reaching there, he killed all of Kichaka's brothers with a single strike, then escaped with Draupadi before anyone could see him. When the king and his soldiers arrived at the cremation ground, they were shocked to find the bodies of Kichaka and his brothers. Meanwhile, Draupadi entered the queen's palace with a smile, terrifying everyone. They began treating her like a goddess. However, Draupadi denied this status and told them to treat her the same as before. News of Kichaka and his brothers' mysterious deaths spread like wildfire across Bharatvarsha. Around the same time, spies of Duryodhana returned to his court,, where Bhishma, Dronacharya, Kripacharya, the Trigarta king Susharma, and Karṇa were seated. They reported that they had failed to locate the Pandavas anywhere—it seemed they were either dead or had become invisible. They also reported the mysterious death of Kichaka and his brothers at the hands of the Gandharvas. Hearing this,

King Susharma felt delighted and suggested conquering the Matsya kingdom, as it had become vulnerable after Kichaka's death. Karṇa agreed. Based on everyone's opinion, Duryodhana also decided to attack the Matsya kingdom. They planned for Trigarta to kidnap the cows from one side, which would engage the Virat army. Meanwhile, the Kuru army would attack from the other side and loot the kingdom. At the end of the 13th year, Susharma captured the cows of the Matsya kingdom and killed the soldiers protecting them. One wounded soldier escaped and informed King Virat. The king immediately prepared his army to counterattack the Trigarta force . Seeing the danger, Kanka (Yudhishthira) advised the king to take Bhima (Vallabh), Nakula (Granthika), and Sahadeva (Arishtanemi) along with him. King Virat agreed. A fierce battle took place between the armies of Matsya and Trigarta. Initially, Trigarta had the upper hand, but with the intervention of the Pandavas, Trigarta was forced to retreat, and Bhima captured King Susharma . After the victory, King Virat sent a soldier back to the city to announce the triumph over Trigarta. However, at that very moment, the Kuru army entered the Matsya kingdom and looted 60,000 cow. The Kuru army was led by Bhishma, Dronacharya, Kripacharya, Ashwatthama, Karṇa, Dushasana, and Shakuni, under the command of Duryodhana. A cowherd, terrified, approached Prince Uttar in the absence of King Virat and told him everything. Though scared after hearing the names of the mighty Kuru warriors . Uttar concealed his fear as he was in the presence of his sister and their servant. To save face, he claimed he could defeat twice the size of the Kuru army but needed a capable charioteer. On hearing this, Brihannala (Arjuna) offered to be his charioteer, but Uttar initially refused. However, Princess Uttara and Brihannala insisted repeatedly, and Uttar had no choice but to accept Brihannala as his charioteer. They then set out toward the location of the Kuru army..

VIRAT WAR

On the battlefield, when Prince Uttar saw Kuru along with its generals, it made him scared to death, so he said to Brihinnala to leave the battlefield. He can't fight those invincible warriors alone. But Brihinala, a.k .a Arjun, tries to motivate him but couldn't succeed in convincing him to fight against enemies. Then he takes Prince Uttar to the tree in the cremation ground where Pandavs hide their weapons & armour. After that, he orders him to take those out from the tree, and then Uttar does as he said. Thereafter, when Uttar bring all the weapons down in front of him, he leaves the woman form and takes Gandhiv, revealing his true identity in front of Uttar. This made Uttar both surprised and happy in the same moment, and he asked for forgiveness for any bad behaviour he or his family had done with them in the past. Then Arjun tightly hugs him and makes him charioteer of his own divine Chariot which he leave in the cremation ground. Thereafter, he, along with Prince Uttar, went to the battlefield where the Kuru army was present. At that time, the mighty Arjuna, the destroyer of enemies, blew his great conch with great force, which made a loud sound. Hearing the sound, the enemies got goosebumps. The sound of that conch, the rattling of the charioteers and the twirling of the Gandiva bow shook the earth. On hearing the great sound of conch, Guru Drona warned Duryodhan about the Arjun and told him about the bad signs that are happening, like the crying of animals pointing toward the sun, etc, and all the soldiers seem to be demotivated.   Thereafter, King Duryodhana said to Bhishma, Drona, and Kripacharya, the great warrior, on the battlefield. We have come here to fight the Matsya residents, not for our selfish reasons, but to help the Trigatas. The Trigartas had described to us the many atrocities committed by the Matsya soldiers. They were very afraid, so we promised to help them. 'Whether this is the king of Matsyas, Virat, or Arjuna has come from his side, then also we all have to fight with him; this is what we have pledged. 'Then why are our best charioteers like Bhishma, Drona, Kripa, Karṇa and Ashwatthama sitting quietly in their chariots with a confused mind? There is no good in anything other than war. Understanding this, we should adapt ourselves to this situation. On hearing Duryodhan's words, Radhanandan Karṇa said, 'King! You should make such a policy by keeping Acharya Drona behind that we can achieve victory. Acharya has always been fond of the Pandavas. Those selfish people have kept Dronacharya with you only to serve their purpose. He says such things that confirm our statement. Thereafter, saying this, Karne started praising himself that he would going burn Arjun just like fire burns the silk. Hearing Karṇa's word, Kripacharya scolded him and reminded him of all the achievements of Arjun that he alone conquered the unconqurable North direct, defeated Devtas in the khandav Forest and killed Nivatkavach, kaljaye, asuras whom even devtas couldn't defeat. Dronacharya and

Ashwatthama also supported him. Then Ashwathaama angrily said to Duryodhan," Just as a hunter earns his living using deceit and fraud, similarly, which wise man, having earned money by deceitful means, will boast of himself? King Duryodhan! Out of the Pandavas whose wealth you have stolen through deceit, when did you defeat Dhananjaya, Nakul or Sahadeva in battle? Which duel was fought in which you defeated Arjuna, etc.? In which battle were you defeated by Dharmaraja Yudhishthira or Bhima, the greatest of the strong? In which battle did you first conquer Indraprastha, which is your possession? Sinners who do evil deeds! Tell me, which war was fought in which you took Draupadi? You people brought the poor Draupadi, who was wearing only one piece of cloth, inside the royal court in her menstrual age, without any reason. Just as Garuda uproots any tree on which he sets his foot with his speed and moves on, similarly, Arjuna, filled with rage, would attack any great warrior on the battlefield and would move ahead only after destroying him. " Then Bhishma interfered between them and said,' This is not the time to oppose each other, especially at such a time when Kunti's son Arjun is present for the war. Respected Acharya Drona and Kripacharya should forgive all the crimes. At this time, we have to fight with Arjuna, the best amongst all weapon holders, on the battlefield. Therefore, the welfare measures followed by the virtuous people of the world should be implemented quickly so that your cattle wealth does not fall into the hands of the enemy. Therefore, O King!

You should either perform your duty in war or act according to Dharma - without a war, give away the kingdom and make peace. Whatever you have to do, do it quickly. Arjuna has now reached your head. He could easily defeat the force of all the 3 worlds, so defeating only the Kuru army is not a big deal for him" But even after hearing everyone's opinion, Duryodhan didn't give up his stubbornness about war against war. Seeing that war is inevitable, he advises Duryodhan to send half of the Kuruksh army to Hastinapur, and they will fight Arjun with half of the army. Everyone agrees with Bhishma 's words and does as he says. Thereafter, Bhishma, the best of the Kurus, created an impenetrable array of all the armies and made it stand in the form of Vajragarbha, Vrihimukh, Ardhachakrantmandal, etc. and behind it, Bhishma also stood with the golden metal flag hoisted and weapons in his hands. At that time, he was looking great. Acharya Drona stand in the middle, Ashvatthama protects the left wing, the Sharadvan Kripa protects the right wing of the army, and Karṇa was at the Frontline. After the Kaurava army was thus formed into a battle formation, Arjuna quickly came near, making all directions resound with the roar of his chariot. The soldiers saw the front of his flag, heard the terrifying sound coming from his chariot and also heard the loud twanging of the Gandiva being pulled. As Arjun came near the army, Drona saw him and praised him, saying, "Kunti's son Arjuna, who lived in the forest and performed penance and valour there, has appeared today. He is saluting me with his first two arrows, and with his second two arrows in my ears, he is asking for permission to fight. Today, after a long time, we have seen Arjuna, the most intelligent person who is loved by his friends and relatives. Oh, Pandava son Dhananjay is shining with his divine Lakshmi (beauty) very brightly. "Arjuna was shining like the scorching sun, approaching; the enemy could not look at him. Seeing the army of charioteers in front, Kuntikumar Arjuna said to Prince Uttar that he was Seeing everyone Drona, Bhishma Karṇa but not Duryodhan he must be hiding in The south part trying to get away with the cow. After that, Arjun went near to Duryodhan's army and started raining arrows on them. These arrows killed many soldiers and created fear among the army of Duryodhan, and then they all ran away, leaving the cow behind. Then Arjun played his conch, which produced a very terrible sound that created chaos among the Kuruksh army and made the cow run toward the south direction of the Matsya Kingdom. When the cows ran towards the capital of Matsyadesh at a great speed and Arjuna, having succeeded in his task, proceeded towards Duryodhan, then the Kaurava warriors, knowing all this, suddenly reached there. When this fierce battle broke out, the greatest warrior of the Kuru clan, ViKarṇa, riding on his chariot, attacked Arjuna by showering a fierce shower of arrows called Vipatha. Then Arjuna, with his arrows, cut off ViKarṇa's bow, which had a strong bow and was studded with gold and called Jambuṇḍa and also broke his flag into pieces and dropped it. After the chariot's flag was cut, ViKarṇa ran away with great speed. Arjuna, who was moving in the Kaurava army, got injured by the arrows of the great charioteer King Shatrutap and immediately pierced him with five arrows. Then Arjun in anger shot his charioteer with ten arrows and sent him to Yamaloka. Arjuna's arrows pierced the armour and entered the body. Wounded by them, King Shatrutap lost his life and fell from the chariot on the battlefield just as a tree uprooted by a storm falls from the mountain peak. Many of the best warriors of the Kaurava army got injured and started trembling after being struck by the arrows of the brave Dhananjaya, just as the trees in the big forests start shaking with the force of a fierce storm according to the time. Just as the strong wind in the spring season blows away the scattered leaves of autumn and shatters the clouds, similarly, the crowned Arjuna, a very brave warrior, sitting on his chariot, roamed around the battlefield, killing his enemies. There was not even a trace of humility in his heart. He was adorned with a beautiful crown and garlands. Sitting on a chariot with red horses, he killed the horses of Karṇa's brother Sangramjit, who came in front of him and also severed his head from the body with an arrow. Karṇa was enraged at the death of his brother Sangramjit, and with a desire to show his valour, he attacked Arjun and Uttara with full force. Seeing his culprit, Karṇa, in front of him, Arjuna's anger flared up. He immediately got filled with joy and enthusiasm and showering fierce arrows, he covered Karṇa along with his horse, chariot and charioteer in a moment. Then the Karṇa, having quickly cut all the arrows shot by Arjun's arms with a group of arrows, began to look beautiful like a fire filled with sparks with his bow and arrows. Then Arjuna too, after afflicting Karṇa with arrows along with his horse, charioteer and chariot, looking at Grandfather Bhishma, Dronacharya and Kripacharya, started a shower of arrows on Karṇa obstinately. Karṇa could not bear Arjuna's prowess. Demonstrating his quickness, he pierced all four of Arjuna's horses with sharp arrows; then, he injured his charioteer with three arrows and, in quick succession, pierced his flag with three arrows. Then, the brave Dhananjaya, with the sharp arrows released from the Gandiva bow, shining like thunderbolts, pierced both the arms, thighs, head, forehead and neck of Karṇa and other excellent body parts. Being struck by the arrows shot by Arjun, the son of Sun, Karṇa was infuriated and, like another powerful elephant defeated by an elephant, he, being distressed by the arrows of Arjun, left the battlefield and fled away. After Radha's son Karṇa fled, the Kaurava warriors, including Duryodhana, along with their armies, slowly advanced towards Pandava's son Arjun. Then, just as the shore of the ocean stops the waves of the ocean, Arjuna, with his battle formation and arrow shower, stopped the advance of the Kaurava army in many parts. The Kaurava army, covered by Arjuna's arrows, looked as beautiful as if the fresh clouds near the mountain had been covered by the rays of the sun. At that time, the Kaurava soldiers, who were bleeding and injured by the arrows of Kunti's son Arjuna, were looking as beautiful as the Ashoka forest covered with many red flowers. Thereafter, the powerful Arjuna, who humbles the enemies, created great fear in the army of Duryodhana by the brilliance of all his weapons, by the sound of his bow, by the terrible noise of the non-human ghosts residing in the flag, by the influence of the extremely terrible roaring monkey and also by the conch that makes a terrible sound. He filled the sky with the bloodthirsty arrows that killed hundreds of enemies and did not even give them a chance to escape or to save themselves. Thereafter, Arjun saw the great warriors of Durypodhan's side and attacked them with his divine weapons. The enemy soldiers could recognize Arjuna's chariot only once when it came near; they never got a chance to do so again because as soon as they came close, Arjuna would send them along with their horses from this world to the other world. The bodies of the Kaurava warriors were torn to pieces after being injured by the arrows of Kunti's son Arjun. They were lying as if they were dead due to the arrows of Partha. He used to cut off the heads of their enemies one by one like grains of rice. Due to the fear of Arjun, all the power of the Kauravas was destroyed. After that, he again gave an introduction of the warriors of Duryodhan's side to Uttara and showed them to him very closely. Then he went toward Kripacharya with full speed. When he reached there, he recited his name and blew his conch, which produced such a loud noise that it triggered the asur residing inside Kripacharya's body, which made him consumed by the hate. Then, in response, Kripacharya also blew the conch and started the duel. Within a moment, their duel became so fierce that even devitas came to see their battle. Thereafter, Arjun, being enraged in that battlefield, shot thirteen arrows as bright as fire at Kripacharya. Then, He cut the yoke of his chariot with one arrow and killed all the four horses with four arrows. With the sixth arrow, he severed the head of the charioteer from his body. When the bow, chariot, horses and charioteer were destroyed, Kripacharya jumped from the chariot to another chariot with a mace in his hand and immediately threw it at Arjuna but he destroys it . Then Arjuna cut off the three venu of the chariot with three arrows, the axle of the chariot with two and the flag of the chariot with the twelfth arrow called Bhalla on the battlefield. After this, Arjuna laughingly injured Kripacharya's chest with the thirteenth arrow, which was like a thunderbolt, leaving him Weapons Less. Seeing this Kaurav army with the fear of Arjun ,takaway Kripa from there and at the same time Dronacharya came in front of Arjun. Then again, a fierce battle happened between them where Arjun wounded Dronacharya so much that Ashwatthama has to intervened in the battle between them, making Dronacharya escape from Arjun to save his (Drona)life. But unlike Dronacharya and Kripacharya, Ashwatthama pierced Arjun with his arrow, making him wounded but couldn't succeed in overcoming him and instead got heavily wounded just like his Father, Dronacharya. Then, seeing this as an opportunity to show his valour, Karna, influenced by Naraksura, went between them and started fighting Arjun. Then Arjun challenges him for a duel, and then Karṇa, accepting his challenge, said, "O son of Kunti, whatever you tell me, show it by doing it. Your words are much more than your actions. This is well known all over the world. Seeing your verbal prowess, we conclude that whatever you have endured in the past, you have done so out of your inability. If you have suffered by being bound in the bondage of Dharma in the past, then even today you are bound in the same way; yet you are considering yourself as if free from that bondage. Even if Indra himself comes to fight for you at this time, I will not feel any pain while showing bravery in the war." Then Arjun laughingly said, "O son of Radha! Only a little while ago, you turned your back on me and fled from the battle; that is why you are still alive, but your younger brother was killed. Who else other than you would be such a man who, after getting his brother killed and even after fleeing from the battlefield, would stand amongst the noble men and brag like this?" Then, Karn angrily attacked Arjun with fierce arrows, but Arjun cut them down with his arrows and inflicted a huge wound on his arms, cutting his bow down. This made Karṇa more angry, and under the influence of Narakasur, he used Shakti against Arjun, but he neutralised it with his power. Meanwhile, many soldiers of Radha's son Karṇa reached there, but Arjun killed them all with the arrows shot by Gandiva bow. Thereafter, Arjun wounded Karṇa's horses with sharp arrows capable of bearing the load (of enemies' blows), which were shot after drawing the bow to the ears. Those horses fell on the ground dead. After that, the mighty Arjun hit Karṇa in the waist with the arrow, burning like fire. That arrow cut through Karṇa's armour and penetrated his chest. This made Karṇa unconscious, and he lost consciousness of anything. Karṇa felt immense pain due to that injury. He left the battlefield and headed towards the north. Seeing him fleeing the battlefield, Arjuna and Uttara, both the great warriors, started roaring, creating fear in the hearts of the enemies. After defeating Karṇa, they went toward Bhishma, where Dusshan and the other kuru brothers stopped Arjun way from reaching toward Bhishma. Then Arjun, without a sweat, made those Kauravs flee from the battlefield. After defeating them, Arjun started massacring the Kuru soldiers by showering fierce arrows on them. In a short while, the entire battlefield was strewn with the bodies of unconscious soldiers. The ground was covered with the corpses of elephant riders, horsemen and men who had fallen from the chariot seats after being killed by sharp arrows. At that time, it seemed as if Arjuna was dancing all around the battlefield with his bow in his hand. The roar of Gandiva was even more powerful than the thunder of the thunderbolt. Hearing it, all the soldiers got frightened and ran away from that great battle. At the mouth of the battle, countless people wearing earrings and turbans were seen lying cut to pieces. Many gold necklaces were lying scattered here and there. The ground was strewn with corpses struck by Arjun's arrows. Many arms had fallen after being cut off, which were still holding bows (firmly in their fists). All the ornaments like armlets, bangles, rings, etc., were intact in those hands. Covered with all these, the battlefield looked very beautiful. At that time, Arjun created a river of blood to flow there, which was very terrifying. Instead of water, a stream of blood flowed in it, and waves of blood arose. Bones were spread in it like a layer of water. It seemed as if death itself had created it during the time of the deluge. Thereafter, seeing Arjun recklessly butchering the kuru army through his arrows, Duryodhana, Karṇa, Dushasana, Vivinshati, Acharya Drona with his son and the great warrior Kripacharya - all these warriors, filled with rage and with the desire to kill Dhananjay, attacked him again, spreading the sound of their strong and strong bows. They surrounded the mighty Dhananjaya (from all sides) and started to attack him with a lot of arrows from their great bows. These three great warriors were raining arrows like the clouds during the rainy season to kill Dhananjaya. Then, Arjun, to counter them, used Endrastra to fill the sky with thunder-like arrows. Just as lightning flashes in the sky when the clouds are raining and illuminates all directions and the earth from all sides, similarly, the Gandiva bow, while raining arrows, completely covered all ten directions. At that time, all the soldiers there, including elephant riders and charioteers, were becoming mesmerized (unconscious). Then Everyone had become numb and mute. No one was in their right senses. All the warriors lost their courage and turned away from the battle. In this way, the entire army formation was broken. All the soldiers despaired of their lives and fled in all directions. Thereafter, Shantanunandan, the famous warrior of the Bharat dynasty grandfather Bhishma, seeing his side's warriors being massacred, ran towards Arjuna. Then Arjun honored Bhishma with an arrow and began the battle by destroying the umbrella of his chariot. This made Bhishma angry, and under the influence of the asur, he started using divine weapons on him, so Arjun also countered it with his divine weapons. This is how a fierce battle started between them, and it became so intense that no kuru soldier or warrior could able to see them even it become even difficult for devtas to conclude who would win this dual. Thereafter, Kunti's son Dhananjaya, who was striving for victory, shot ten arrows into the chest of the mighty Bhishma, causing deep injury. Being troubled by this, Bhishma remained sitting motionless for a long time holding the chariot's hump. He was unconscious. Remembering the advice that 'In such a situation, the charioteer must protect the charioteer', the charioteer who was controlling the chariot and horses took the great warrior Bhishma away from the battlefield to save his life. When Bhishma left the battle front and moved away, Duryodhana, hoisting the flag of his chariot and taking up bow in his hand and roaring, attacked Arjun. But Arjun, in no time wounded him very badly made his armour cover with blood. Duryodhan, being wounded heavily, went in a different direction, away from Arjun. Seeing this, the crown-wearing Arjuna clapped his hands and, with enthusiasm for the battle in his heart, began to challenge the enemy and said, "Son of Dhritarashtra! Why are you running away from the battle? Oh! By doing this, you have lost your fame and great glory. Today, your victory celebrations are not being celebrated like before. I, the third Pandava, am standing for the battle, obedient to the same King Yudhishthira whom you have dethroned. Therefore, turn back and show your face to me. Remember what a king's conduct should be like. In vain, you were named Duryodhan on this earth. You are running away from the war; hence you do not have any quality here to match the name Duryodhan" When Arjun challenged him for battle in this manner, Duryodhan, son of Dhritarashtra, being struck by the goad of his harsh words, turned back like a mad elephant. Seeing him return, Karṇa, too, somehow managed to recover his injured body and returned and, staying on the northern (left) side of Duryodhan, went to face Partha in the battlefield. After that, Drona, Kripacharya, Bhishma, Vivinshati and Dushasan also came soon. With their huge bows pointed, they all came with great haste from the east or front to protect Duryodhana. These great warriors surrounded Arjun from all sides and started attacking him with arrows. Then Arjun dispelled their arrows with his divine weapons and took up sammonhan astra and merged it with his conch. After that, Kuntikumar held his great conch with both hands and blew it, which made a terrifying sound and could be heard from a long distance. Its sound reverberated in all directions, in the sky and on the earth. All those Kaurava warriors were mesmerized (smell away) by the sound of that conch shell blown by Arjuna, and all of them, abandoning their rare bows, were immersed in deep peace (unconsciousness). After all the warriors had gone into a deep sleep, Arjun said prince uttar should take away the clothes of all the warriors except Bhishma because he was still in his conscious state. As Prince Uttar went to take clothes, Bhishma attacked Arjun , Then Arjun first killed his horse and then pierced him with 10 arrows, making his body like a Porcupine. After that, he traps his chariot with arrows, making him unable to move. Thus, after taking away the cloths of all the kuru warriors except Bhishma Arjun along with Prince Uttar, they returned to the Matsya kingdom. Where Prince gifted that cloth to his sister and told her the true identity of Pandavs. And finally, after the end of 13 years, Pandavs vanvaas got over, and they revealed their true identity to King Virat. After that, King Virat offered his daughter's hand to Arjun, but he refused to marry her and made his son Abhimanyu marry Princess Uttara, making her his daughter-in-law.

TALK FOR PEACE

After the the exile period of Pandavs, both Kaurav and Pandav began gathering for the war. Shree Krishna himself went to Pandav's side as Arjun's charioteer and gave his Narayani Sena to Durayodhan. After both sides assembled their armies along with their respective kings. King Dhritarashtra, on the advice of Mahatma Vidura, sent Sanjaya as a messenger of peace to the Matsya Kingdom to calm down the Pandavas. However, he failed in his mission. Instead the Pandavas sent him back to Hastinapur with a message demanding the return of their kingdom. Thereafter, Sanjaya returned to Hastinapur and conveyed Yudhishthira's message to the king in the royal assembly, also giving a brief description of the Pandavas' army. Hearing about Pandav's power, Drithrasthra get worried and tried to convince Duryodhan to return Pandav's kingdom. Bhishma joined him in persuading Duryodhana, but he did not listen. Instead, he began praising himself and Karṇa, claiming that both of them alone could defeat the Pandavas along with their armies using a single chariot. Thereafter, Karṇa also joins him in self-praising and declared that they didn't need Bhishma or Dronacharya; he alone can kill Pandavs. Upon hearing Karṇa's arrogant words, Bhishma angrily said, ""Death has clouded your wisdom. Don't you know that if you, the chief warrior, are killed in battle, all the sons of Dhritarashtra will be as good as dead? The power that

Mahendra, the king of devtas, gave you will be shattered and burned in battle when it is struck by the chakra driven by Bhagwan Keshava. You will witness it with your own eyes. The serpent-faced arrow you worship with garlands and reverence will be shattered by the arrows of Arjuna, son of Pandu, and perish with you " Bhishma's words angered Karṇa, and he threw down his weapons in front of everyone, declaring that he would only enter the battlefield after Bhishma's death, and then he stormed out of the assembly hall. After Karṇa left, Bhishma told Dhritarashtra that Karṇa was one of the major reasons behind Duryodhana's evil mindset. He advised the king to expel both of them from the kingdom. However, because of his emotional attachment to Duryodhana, Dhritarashtra ignored Bhishma's advice and again tried to convince Duryodhana, who still refused to listen and walked out of the court. Seeing the certainty of a bloody war, Dhritarashtra again sent Sanjaya to the Pandavas, but the attempt failed. Similarly, King Yudhishthira sent a well-educated Brahmin as a peace messenger to Hastinapur, but Duryodhana rejected that message too. Even sages like Vyasa, Maitreya, Parashurama, and Brahmarishi Narada tried to persuade him to abandon hostility toward the Pandavas, but he refused to listen and remained firm on the idea of war. When all peace efforts failed, Shree Krishna decided to go to Hastinapur himself as a messenger from the Pandavas. He went along with Satyaki. Duryodhana himself received him along with his companions and offered him to stay at

Dushasana's house. Knowing the Kauravas' hatred toward him, Krishna refused and chose to stay at Vidura's house. There, he met Mata Kunti and took her blessings. Vidura warned Krishna about Duryodhana's evil intent to kill the Pandavas and also cautioned him that Duryodhana might try to imprison him. Listening to Vidura's concerns, Krishna reassured him and said that even if all the kings united against him, they could not harm him. After consoling Vidura, he went to sleep. The next day, he went to the royal court to deliver his message to King Dhritarashtra. At the palace gates, Dushasana greeted him respectfully and escorted him to the court, where everyone honored him and offered him a golden seat. Great sages also arrived to witness his presence. Once seated in the court, Krishna conveyed the Pandavas' message and offered a compromise — to give the Pandavas just five villages. But Duryodhana, consumed by hatred, rejected even this humble offer. Enraged, he left the court with his ministers. Krishna then suggested to King Dhritarashtra that if he truly wished for peace in Bharatvarsha, he should imprison Duryodhana. Hearing this, Duryodhana's anger intensified. In a meeting with his inner circle, Karṇa suggested they imprison Krishna instead. Duryodhana liked the idea and returned to the court to execute the plan. Then ,Satyaki, who could read a person's mind through gestures, sensed Duryodhana's evil intentions. Therefore, He ordered Kritavarma to station an army outside the court and warned Krishna of the plan. Hearing Satyaki's warning, Mahatma Vidura became furious and rebuked Duryodhana for his self-destructive behavior. He not only scolded him but also reminded everyone of Krishna's divinity and that no one in the universe was superior to him. Upon hearing this, Krishna said to Duryodhana - "You foolish Duryodhan! Due to your attachment, you are considering me alone, and therefore, you are trying to capture me by insulting me. This is your ignorance. 'Look, all the Pandavas are here. The heroes of the Andhaka and Vrishni clans are also present here. Adityas, Rudras and Vasus, along with Maharishis, are also here".

Saying this, Bhagwan Keshav, the destroyer of opposing heroes, laughed loudly. As he laughed, the deities present in the limbs of Mahatma Shri Krishna—whose light was like lightning and whose body was as small as a thumb—started emitting flames of fire. Brahma appeared in his forehead, and Rudradev appeared in his chest. All the Lokpals were situated in his arms. Flames of fire came out of his mouth. Aditya, Sadhya, Vasu, both Ashwinikumars, Indra along with the Marudgan, Vishvedev, Yaksha, Gandharva, Naga, and Rakshasas also appeared in his various body parts. Balarama and Arjuna were born from his two arms. Arjuna, the archer, appeared in his right arm, and Balarama, the wielder of the plough, in his left. . Conch, Chakra, Mace, Shakti, Sharpshooting bow, Plough, and the sword named Nandak—these weapons shone brilliantly in the many arms of Shri Krishna when he raised them.

From his eyes, nostrils, and ears, smoky flames of fire appeared everywhere. Seeing that terrifying form of Mahatma Shri Krishna, all the kings were filled with fear and closed their eyes. Except for Bhishma ,Dronacharya, the most intelligent Vidur, the great fortunate Sanjaya and the sages who were rich in penance, everyone else closed their eyes. God himself had given divine vision to Drona and others so they could see him. Seeing the most amazing form of Shri Krishna in the assembly hall, the bells of the Devas rang, and flowers rained down. At that moment, King Dhritarashtra also asked Bhagwan for divine eyes to witness his divine form. Bhagwan Vasudev granted him divine sight. When Dhritarashtra, seated on the throne, regained his sight, all the kings and sages were astonished and began praising Madhusudan. At that moment, the entire earth shook, the sea roared, and all the kings were greatly surprised. Then Lord Krishna returned to his normal state, gathering his divine power within himself.

After that, with the permission of the sages, Madhusudan left the assembly along with Satyaki and Kritvarma. As soon as he left, the Maharshis like Narada also disappeared, and all the noise faded. It was a wonderful event. As Shri Krishna departed, the Kauravas and the kings followed him, but Shri Krishna, ignoring the king's orders, walked out of the hall like a smoky fire and went to prepare his chariot to return to the Pandavas. Knowing that Shri Krishna's chariot was ready and he was about to leave, King Dhritarashtra said to him. " Shatrusudan Janardan! You can see how much my power works on my sons. Everything is in front of your eyes; nothing is hidden from you. I, too, wish that there should be a treaty between the Kauravas and the Pandavas, and I keep making efforts for this; but considering my condition, you should not doubt me. " Thereafter, the mighty-armed Shri Krishna said to King Dhritarashtra, Acharya Drona, Grandfather Bhishma, Vidur, Bahika and Kripacharya ", You all witnessed what happened in the Kaurava Sabha. How the foolish Duryodhana stormed out in anger like a rude man. Maharaja Dhritarashtra himself admits his inability to stop Duryodhan. So now I seek your permission—I will go to Yudhishthira." After that sitting on the chariot, the great archer and excellent warrior of Bharat dynasty followed him for some distance. After that, sitting on the chariot. After that, Shri Krishna sat on his chariot. The great archer and excellent warrior of the Bharat dynasty followed him for some distance.

CONVERSATION

After Shree Krishna reached the border of Hastinapur, every warrior of the Kuru clan returned to their respective places except Karṇa, who accompanied him a bit further beyond the boundaries of Hastinapur. Shree Krishna, knowing that Narakasura resided inside Karṇa's body and that Karṇa was the chief adviser and best friend of Duryodhan, told him the truth about his birth and offered him the kingdom of the Pandavas. But Karṇa, politely rejecting his offers said that he could not leave his parents who had raised him in the best possible way and had given him a luxurious life by getting him married to many beautiful women.

भार्याश्चोढा मम प्राप्ते यौवने तत्परिग्रहात् ॥ १० ॥
तासु पुत्राश्च पौत्राश्च मम जाता जनार्दन । तासु मे हृदयं
कृष्ण संजातं कामबन्धनम् ॥ ११ ॥

"Shri Krishna! When I reached my youth, Adhiratha got me married to several women of the Suta caste. Now, I even have sons and grandsons from them. O Janardana! My heart has been attached to those women with feelings of desire

(Udyog parva ,Bhagvadyana Parva, chap 141 , shloka 10 &11)

Whereas Mata Kunti had abandoned him in the river. Duryodhan entirely depends on him in this war; he can't leave him. Thereafter Karṇa said that they (he, Duryodhan Dusashan and Shakuni) had done a lots of sins so the only way for their salvation left is to die in this great war of Dharma. Then, Shree Krishna laughingly said, "Karṇa! It seems that the method I am telling you to acquire the kingdom is not acceptable to you. You do not want to rule the earth given to you by me. The victory of the Pandavas is inevitable. There is no doubt about this also. That terrible victory flag presented by Pandanu Nandan Arjuna to the monkey king Hanuman appears very high. Karṇa! When you will see Arjuna, the white vehicle, who has come with me as the charioteer of Shri Krishna in the war, manifesting the Andra, Agneya and Vayavya weapons and when Gandiva's thunderous sound like the thunder of the thunderbolt will sound in your ears, at that time you will not believe in Satyayuga, Treta and Dwapara (only the fierce Kali in the form of discord) will be visible. When you see mighty Bhimasena dancing in the war after drinking Dushasan's blood and destroying the enemy's elephant army like an intoxicated elephant, you will no longer feel the presence of Satya Yuga, Treta Yuga, or Dwapara Yuga. Tell Bhishma, Dronacharya, and Kripacharya, 'Seven days from today, there will be Amavasya. Its deity is said to be Indra. The war must begin on that day.' Similarly, tell all the kings gathered for war, 'Whatever desire you hold in your heart, I shall fulfill it.' All the kings and princes under

Duryodhan's command will attain the highest goal by dying in battle.. "After listening to Shree Krishna's words, Karṇa shared the bad omens he had observed, which indicated defeat. He also told him about a dream in which he had seen Bhishma, Dronacharya, Duryodhan, and himself traveling southward on a camel-driven chariot — a sign of death. After that, he said that he, along with every king fighting for Duryodhan, would burn in the fire of Gandiva.

अहं चान्ये च राजानो यच्च तत् क्षत्रमण्डलम् ।
गाण्डीवाग्नि प्रवेक्ष्याम इति मे नास्ति संशयः

I and all these kings, and this entire Kshatriya circle,
Shall enter the fire of Gandiva — of this I have no doubt.

(Udyoga parva ,Bhagvadyana Parva, chap 143, shloka 45)

After that, Shree Krishna said, "Karṇa! Surely the time of destruction of this earth has arrived; that is why my words do not reach your heart. When the destruction of all beings is near, then even injustice appears like justice and cannot go out of the heart" Then, Karṇa ended the conversation and said,"Shri Krishna! If I survive this great war that destroys the valiant kshatriyas, I will see you again, or we will meet in heaven; this is certain. Anagh! There we will meet again like today".Saying this, Karṇa embraced Lord Krishna, bid him farewell, and got down from the rear side of the chariot. Thereafter,

Karṇa went back to Hastinapur, and Shree Krishna went ahead with his journey.

Upon entering Hastinapur, Karṇa stopped to perform Surya Vandana, and at the same time, Mata Kunti came to him and asked him to take the Pandavas' side. She told him about his birth story. But Narakasura, within Karṇa, knowing how his empire had ended after he disrespected Mata Aditi, took control over Karṇa's personality and respectfully promised her that he would not kill all her sons but only Arjuna — so that she would still have her five sons alive. Karṇa's (Narakasura's) promise made Mata Kunti feel satisfied and sad at the same time. After that, she went back home with tears in her eyes. Thereafter, even Dhritarashtra, Bhishma, Dronacharya, and every other elder again tried to convince Duryodhana, but they all failed. At last, war became inevitable, and the armies of both sides set up their tents around Kurukshetra, where they were going to fight the bloodiest and biggest war in the history of mankind.

Notes: Many scholars, in order to defend Karṇa's evil actions, argued that he was a good person — that was why he accepted his sins in front of Shree Krishna. But they forgot that he was standing before Shree Krishna, whose mere presence could diminish the Rajasik and Tamasik qualities of the heart and make it purely Sattvik. As mentioned in the Śrīmad Bhāgavatam, 10th Skandha, Chapter 4: Kaṁsa, the most cruel king of that era, asked Vasudeva and Devaki to forgive his sins due to the divine aura of Shree Krishna residing within them. But once that aura diminished, he regained his cruelty and again imprisoned them . In the same way, due to the presence of Shree Krishna himself, Karṇa became Sattvik, accepted his sins, and even wished for the victory of the Pāṇḍavas. But as soon as Shree Krishna left, he once again regained his older nature — full of ego, envy, and hatred

ARMIES OF BOTH SIDES

After settling in the Kurushetra, both Pandav and Kaurav start their preparation for war. King Yudhisthir, with the advice of Shree Krishna, declares Dristhaduymna as his commander-in-chief, whereas Duryodhan makes Bhishma his commander-in-chief. Thereafter, becoming commander in chief of the Kuru army, Bhishma assure Duryodhan that he will fight against the Pandavas with his full power and that not even devas could make them win this battle. This made Duryodhan glad, and he asked, "O son of Kuru! You know the number of charioteers and charioteers of the enemy and your side completely, so I also want to get information about this matter from you; because the grandfather is well versed in the knowledge of all the things of the enemy and his side, so I want to hear this matter from your mouth along with all these kings. " Then Bhishma replies, "The number of charioteers in your army reaches thousands, lakhs and crores; however, listen to me about the names of the chief among them. First of all, you are a very generous charioteer along with your hundred brothers like Dushasan, etc. Kritavarma of Bhojvanshi, the best among the armed men, is the bravest among your group. He will achieve your desired goal in the war. There is no doubt about this. Even the greatest experts in warfare cannot defeat him. I also consider the great archer Madraraja Shalya as an Atirathi, who always competes with Lord Krishna in every battle. I consider Shalya, the bravest of your army, to be a great warrior. He will fight like the waves of the ocean, drowning the enemy soldiers with his arrows. The great archer Bhurishrava, son of Somdutt, is also a scholar of weapons and a well-wisher of yours. He is also the commander of the charioteers. Hence, he will cause great destruction to the army of your enemies. I consider Sindhuraj Jaydrath to be equal to two charioteers. He is very valiant and the best among charioteers. O King! He will also fight with the Pandavas on the battlefield. King Sudakshin of Kamboja country is considered a charioteer. He will fight with the enemies on the battlefield to ensure the success of your task. This Kambojaraja, who is as valiant as a lion among charioteers, will display valour like that of Indra in the war for you, and all the Kauravas will see his valour. King Neel, a resident of Mahishmatipuri, is also a charioteer in your army. He is wearing blue armour. He will destroy the enemies with his chariot force. Both the brave princes of Avantidesh, Vind and Anuvind, are considered to be the best charioteers. They are the expert in the art of war and are endowed with strength and bravery. I consider the five brothers from Trigarta country to be generous charioteers. During the battle of Virat nagar, their enmity with the four Pandavas had increased. These five brothers are charioteers, and Satyarath is the charioteer among them. O Bharata!

Remembering the earlier enmity that Bhimasena's younger brother, the white-horsed Arjuna, had shown towards the Trigartas during his conquest of the world, these five brave men will fight with full concentration on the battlefield. Your son Lakshmana and Dushasan's son, these two lion-men, are not going to flee from the war. These two are not only brave charioteers, they are also the best among charioteers. They will perform great feats in the war by being devoted to Kshatriya Dharma. King Brihadbal of Kosala, who is endowed with great speed and valour, is also a charioteer in my view. His place among charioteers is very high. Sharadwan's son, Kripacharya, is the leader of charioteers. He will burn your enemies without caring for his own dear life. O king! This uncle of yours, Shakuni, is a charioteer. There is no doubt that he will take up the fight against the Pandavas. The great archer Drona's son, Ashwatthama, is greater than all the archers. He faces the enemies in a strange way in the war, is equipped with strong weapons and is a master. The greatness of this brave man, the best among charioteers, cannot be calculated. If this great charioteer wants, he can burn the three worlds. Ashwatthama's father, Dronacharya, is a very brilliant person. Even though he is old, he is better than the young men. I have no doubt that he will display his great valour in this war. Dronacharya standing firm in the battlefield is like fire. He will be aroused by the support of the wind in the form of weapons and will become aflame by getting the straw and fuel in the form of the army. In this way, by becoming aflame, he will burn the armies of Yudhishthira, son of Pandu, to ashes. King! The great king Paurav in your army is, in my opinion, a great charioteer among the great charioteers. He is capable of giving trouble to the brave charioteers of the opposition. Prince Brihadbal is also a charioteer; his true fame has spread in the world. He will roam like death in the army of your enemies. Karṇa's son, Vrishasena, is also a great charioteer in your army. He can also be called a Maharathi. The best of the strong, Vrishasena, will destroy the huge army of your enemies. The mighty Jalasandh is the best charioteer in your army. He will even sacrifice his life for you in the war. King Bahrik is a great warrior. He never retreats from the battle. King! I consider him a warrior better than Yamraj on the battlefield. The cruel demon king Alambusha is also a great warrior. O King! Remembering the past enmity, he will kill the enemies. King Bhagdatta of Pragjyotishpur is very brave and majestic. He holds the highest rank among the braves who control elephants with the goad in his hand. He is also skilled in chariot fighting. ”

Thereafter, pointing toward Karṇa Bhishma said to Duryodha, “King! This dear friend of yours, Karṇa, who always encourages you to fight with the Pandavas and always displays his cruelty in the battlefield, is very harsh-spoken, self-praising and mean. This Karṇa has become your minister, leader and friend. He is arrogant and has climbed very high after getting your shelter. This Karṇa is neither a great charioteer nor is he worthy of being called a charioteer in the battlefield because this fool has lost his natural armour and divine earrings. He always has a feeling of hatred towards others. Due to the curse of Parshuramji, the curse of the Brahmin and the loss of the above-mentioned equipment that can ensure victory, in my view, this Karṇa is a half charioteer. He can never survive when he fights with Arjun. He shows a lot of pride in every battle but is always seen running away from there. Karṇa is kind and careless. Hence, in my opinion also he is Ardha Rathi" On hearing this Karṇa started looking at Bhishma with red eyes in anger and while tormenting him with the whip of his words, he said to Bhishma "Although I have not done any crime against you, yet because of your hatred towards me you keep hurting me with your words at every step as per your wish. I silently endure all this for the sake of Duryodhan, but you consider me a fool and a coward. The opinion that you are making about me being a half-warrior will undoubtedly appear so to the entire world because everyone knows that Ganganandan Bhishma does not lie. You always harm the Kauravas, but King Duryodhan does not understand this. The way you want to make the kings turn away from me because of your hatred towards my qualities, who else can make such an effort except you? At this time, the occasion of war has come, and kings of equal rank with generous character have gathered; on such an occasion, who will destroy the brilliance and enthusiasm of the warriors of his own side by wishing to create differences among them? One should listen to the words of elders; this is the order of the scriptures. But those who have become very old are not worth listening to because they are considered to be like children again. The best! I will single-handedly destroy the Pandavas' army in this war, but all the fame will go to Bhishma. You have made Bhishma the commander. The glory of victory is received only by the commander; it is not received by the warriors in any way. So Rajan! I will not fight any war as long as Bhishma is alive, but after Bhishma is killed, I will compete with all the great warriors. " Then Bhishma angrily replies to him, "O son of a charioteer! In this war, I have borne the burden of Duryodhan, which is as huge as the ocean, on my shoulders. The painful and thrilling time for which I had been worried for many years has now come. In such a situation, I should not create this mutual difference. That is why you are still alive. If this were not the case, then even though I am old, I would have displayed my valour and destroyed both your faith in war and your hope for life. Jamadagni's son Parashurama used big weapons on me, but even they could not cause me any pain. Then what can you do to me? You are the embodiment of enmity. With your support, a great injustice has occurred for the destruction of the Kuru clan. Now, you make arrangements for their protection and show your bravery. " Thereafter, Duryodhan stopped both of them and requested Bhishma to tell them about the chief warriors of Pandav's side. Therefore, on the request of Duryodhan Bhishma starts telling about Pandav's side warrior:" King Yudhishthir, the son of Pandu, who enhances Kuntika's happiness, is a great charioteer. There is no doubt that he will spread everywhere like fire in the battlefield. King! Bhimsen alone is equal to eight charioteers. There is no other warrior equal to him in the battle fought with mace and arrows. He has the strength of ten thousand elephants. He is very proud and is blessed with supernatural brilliance. Both the sons of Madri are as handsome and bright as the Ashwini Kumars. Both of them are best among Charioteers. These four brothers, remembering the great troubles you them, will enter your army and roam around killing people like Bhagwan Rudra; I have no doubt about this. Shri Krishna in the form of Narayana is the friend and helper of Arjuna who conquers sleep with red eyes. There is no other brave charioteer like Arjun in both the armies of Kaurava and Pandava. There is no one like Arjuna among all the devtas, danav, serpents, rakshas and Yakshas; then how can there be any among humans? I have not heard of any such charioteer in the past or the future. Dhrishtadyumna, the master disciple of Dronacharya, who is the commander of the entire army of Pandavas, is superior, in my opinion. Just as Rudra Dev, holding Pinaka, gets angry and kills people during the time of destruction, similarly, he will fight in this war, killing his enemies. In my understanding, Dhrishtadyumna's son Kshatradharma is still a half-warrior. Being a child, he has not put much effort into the art of weapons. Shishupala's brave son, the great archer Chediraj Dhrishtaketu Pandunandan, is a relative of Yudhishthir and a great expert. The Kshatriya-devout Kshatradev, who conquers the enemy cities, is, in my opinion, the best charioteer of the Pandava army. Jayant, Amitauja and the mighty warrior Satyajit - all of them are great warriors of Panchala, great-minded and brave warriors. All of them will fight on the battlefield like an angry elephant. For the Pandavas, the powerful warriors Aja and Bhoj are both great warriors. They will fight with all their might and will prove their valour. The Kekaya princes, who wield weapons swiftly, are valiant warriors, adept in warfare and have great courage; they are all considered generous charioteers. Their flags are all red in colour. All these warriors, named Sukumar, Kashik, Neel, Suryadatta, and Shankha Madirashwa, are generous charioteers. Maharaj! I consider Vardhakshim to be a great charioteer, and in my opinion, King Chitrayudha is the best charioteer. Chitrayudha is the most beautiful warrior in the battle and is a devotee of Arjuna. Chekitana and Satyadhriti - these two lion-men are the great charioteers of the Pandava army. I consider them the best among charioteers. Vyaghradatta and Chandrasen - these two kings are also the best charioteers of Pandavas army in my opinion. Another name of King Senabindu is Krodhahanta. O Lord! He is considered to be as valiant as Lord Krishna and Bhimasena. He will fight with your soldiers on the battlefield, displaying his valour. In my view, the king of Kashi who conquered the enemy city should be considered as a charioteer in his normal state, but at the time when they start displaying bravery in battle, they should be considered equal to eight charioteers. Drupada's young son, Satyajit, is always eager for war. He has attained the status of Atirathi, just like Dhrishtadyumna. He will perform great deeds in the war with the desire to expand the fame of the Pandavas. The mighty Pandya king, a valiant warrior from the Pandava side, is another great warrior. He is fond of the Pandavas and is a brave warrior. His bow is huge and strong. He is a respected warrior in the Pandava army. King Shreniman and Vasudan- both of them are considered to be very brave warriors. They are capable of conquering the enemy's city. King Rochman is a great warrior on the Pandava side. He will fight the enemy army in the war showing valour like that of the devtas. Kuntibhojkumar King Purujit, who is the maternal uncle of Bhimsen, is also a great archer and very strong. I also consider him as Atirathi. The valiant Purujit will readily perform great deeds in the war for his nephews, who are dear to him, and in the interest of the Pandavas. The rakshas king Ghatotkacha, son of Bhimsen and Hidimba, is very elusive. In my opinion, he is also the commander of charioteers. He loves fighting very much. That illusionary Rakshas will fight enthusiastically in the battlefield. The brave rakshas and secretaries who are with him will all remain under his control. Rajan! These are the main charioteers, extra charioteers and half charioteers of Mahatma Pandu Nandan Yudhishthira. Nareshwar! These above-mentioned heroes will lead the battle of Yudhishthira's fearsome army, protected by the brave Arjuna, who is crowned with the brilliance of Indra. " Thereafter discussing the warriors from both the sides, they made their strategy for the next day and went to their respective tents.

THE TEN DAYS

On the first day of the war, both the Kuru and Pandava armies gathered in front of each other. Before the war began, King Yudhisthir, along with the Pandavas, went to Bhishma, Dronacharya, and Kripacharya to take their blessings. Seeing such a gesture from King Yudhisthir, the soldiers on both sides praised him. Thereafter, the war began, and Bhishma started massacring the Pandava army. No one could stop him. But King Virat's elder son, Shwet, gave him a tough duel, and everyone felt that he was going to kill Bhishma. However, Bhishma used a divine weapon and killed him, terrifying Yudhisthir's entire army. Seeing his army in panic, Yudhisthir pulled them back, ending the first day of the war with a victory for Duryodhan's side.

On the second day of the war, the Kalinga army surrounded Bhimsen alone in an attempt to kill him. But Bhimsen, with a single sword, massacred more than half of the Kalinga army, killing major Kalinga warriors including Bhanuman, Satya, Ketuman, and others. On the other hand, Abhimanyu displayed great valour on the battlefield against powerful warriors. Arjun also came to support him in the battle. Seeing Arjun alone with Abhimanyu, Bhishma, Drona, and Kripa surrounded them, but none of them could defeat Arjun. Arjun, along with Shree Krishna, killed everyone who came in front of him with his fierce arrows. This made the Kaurava soldiers afraid. Observing their condition,

Bhishma, on Dronacharya's advice, pulled their army back, concluding the second day of the war with a victory for the Pandavas

Again, at the beginning of the 3rd day, a fierce battle took place between both sides. Bhimsen, Ghatotkacha, and Satyaki made the Kuru army flee, terrorizing them to the core. Seeing this, Bhishma and Dronacharya moved forward to stop them, but Arjun blocked their way and started butchering the Kuru army with his own forces. Meanwhile, Bhimsen and Ghatotkacha, the father-son duo, showed tremendous valor and cut through the Kaurava army like vegetables. Then, Bhimsen, upon seeing Duryodhan, angrily pierced his chest and made him lose consciousness. His charioteer then took him away from Bhimsen. Seeing Duryodhan unconscious, the Kuru army fell into chaos. On the other hand, Dhrishtadyumna and Yudhishthir chased the Kaurava army away; even Bhishma and Dronacharya were unable to control the situation. Later, Duryodhan regained consciousness. Seeing his army in such a terrible condition, he asked Bhishma to fight with his full strength against the Pandavas; otherwise, he said, there was no point in continuing the war. Listening to this, the Asura inside Bhishma took over, suppressing his soft corner for the Pandavas. After that, he revealed his fierce form to the Pandavas and burned their army with arrows, just as fire burns cotton. Shree Krishna, who had vowed not to fight in the war, saw Bhishma massacring the Pandava army and rushed forward to kill him. But Arjun stopped him, convincing him that he would fight with his full potential. Then, Arjun stood before the Kuru army like a lion before a group of deer. With the string of his Gandiva, he created a terrible sound that filled the hearts of enemies with fear. After that, he rained arrows on the Kuru army, creating a huge river of Duryodhan's slain soldiers. Using Indrastra, he wounded all the warriors, including Bhishma and Dronacharya, covering their bodies with blood,Thus, Bhishma, seeing his army scattered in fear and his warriors heavily wounded, withdrew his forces, concluding the victory of the Pandavas on the 3rd day of the war.

On the fourth day of the war, Abhimanyu showed great valor in the battlefield. Thereafter, Drishtadyumna also joined him, and Shalya, along with his son, attacked them. Drishtadyumna killed the son of Shalya. This made Shalya very angry, and he hit Drishtadyumna with arrows, but this did not affect him. A ferocious duel started between them, in which Drishtadyumna wounded Shalya with his arrows. Meanwhile, the Kauravas surrounded Abhimanyu in an attempt to capture him, but Bhimsen came between them. Upon seeing Duryodhana, Bhimsen got down from his chariot with his mace in hand and started massacring the Kuru army. The elephant army of Magadha tried to stop him, but he killed all of them alone with his mace. Thereafter, Bhishma came to stop him, but Satyaki intervened, preventing Bhishma and other warriors from reaching

Bhimsen. Then Bhimsen got back on his chariot and went towards the Kaurava group, where he alone fought the fourteen brothers of Duryodhana and killed five of them, making the rest flee .Then Bhagadatta, seeing Bhimsen killing the Kuru army, started attacking him and soon overcame him. Seeing his father being overpowered by Bhagadatta, Ghatotkacha joined him and defeated Bhagadatta, massacring the Kuru army. Seeing that there was no stopping Ghatotkacha, Bhishma withdrew the army, declaring a win for the Pandavas on the fourth day of the war.

On the 5th day, a fierce battle took place between the two sides. Bhimsen went directly against Bhishma, and a destructive battle followed between them, destroying everything around. However, it did not lead to any conclusion, so both of them went in different directions. Bhishma went against King Virat, Arjun fought Ashwatthama, Duryodhan battled Bhimsen, and Abhimanyu clashed with Lakshman. In these duels, Bhishma massacred the Virat army, and Arjun fought Ashwatthama but later spared him, considering him his guru's son and a Brahmin. Meanwhile, Bhimsen and Abhimanyu forced both father and son—Duryodhan and Lakshman—to flee from the battlefield. At the same time, Bhurishrava alone killed ten sons of Satyaki and also destroyed Satyaki's chariot, making him flee. This enraged Arjun, and he burned an army of fifty thousand warriors just like fire burns moths.

Thereafter, Abhimanyu came to accompany his father. At that very moment, the sun moved westward, casting delusion over all the Kuru soldiers. Seeing this, Bhishma withdrew his army once again, declaring victory of the Pandavas for the 5th day of the wa.

On the 6th day of the war, Bhimsen alone went inside the enemy's army, and soon the Kauravas surrounded him from all sides. Seeing this, Bhimsen took his mace, got down from the chariot, and started attacking his enemies. He alone killed many Rathis, elephants, and horses with the movement of his mace. Thereafter, the Kauravas surrounded him and started attacking him with every weapon. Then Drishtadyumna came there to help him, and Bhimsen got back on his chariot. Together, both of them started massacring the Kuru army. Then Dronacharya came there but was unable to stop them. Thereafter, Duryodhan also came, but Bhimsen, with a single arrow, pierced his chest, making him unconscious. This created chaos in the Kuru army, and even Bhishma was unable to stop it. On the other hand, Arjun, along with Shree Krishna, Bhimsen, and Drishtadyumna, chased the Kuru army just like a lion chases a group of deer. Therefore, Bhishma withdrew his army, declaring the victory of the Pandavas at the end of the 6th day of the war.

At the beginning of the 7th day of the war, Duryodhan requested Bhishma to defeat the Pandavas once and for all, as they were becoming more fierce day by day.

Bhishma replied that even though defeating the Pandavas was impossible, he would still try his best in that day's battle. When the war began, Bhishma directly engaged Arjuna, but their battle did not come to any conclusion, so they moved in different directions. Meanwhile, Dronacharya fought Virat, Ashwatthama faced Shikandi, Nakul and Sahadev fought Shalya, Bhagadatta fought Ghatochkacha, Satyaki battled the Rakshasa king Alambusha, Drishtadyumna engaged Duryodhan, and Bhimsen fought Kritavarma. Dronacharya killed Virat's son Shanka, causing King Virat to flee from the battlefield. Bhimsen and Drishtadyumna defeated Duryodhan and Kritavarma. A fierce battle also took place between Bhagadatta and Ghatochkacha, where Bhagadatta nearly killed Ghatochkacha, but the latter somehow managed to save his life. Having gained the upper hand, Bhagadatta created chaos in the Pandava army and chased them away. On the other hand, Satyaki defeated the Rakshasa king Alambusha, which motivated the Pandava soldiers to fight. However, Dronacharya and Bhishma soon arrived at the scene, ending their motivation and chasing them away. Seeing his army disheartened, King Yudhishthira withdrew his forces from the battlefield, thereby declaring the victory of the Kauravas at the end of the seventh day of the war

On the eighth day of the war, Bhishma showed great valour, raining arrows on the Pandava army and killing thousands of soldiers at once. On seeing Bhishma killing the soldiers of his side, Bhimsen went against him, killed Bhishma's horses, cut down his bow, and killed his charioteer. Therefore, nine brothers of Duryodhan came to rescue Bhishma, but soon Bhimsen killed all of them in front of Bhishma. This traumatised Duryodhan, so he went to Bhishma and requested him to kill the Pandavas, as it made him very sad to see his brothers dying in front of him. Then, Bhishma, repeating his words, said that not even Indra with his divine army could defeat the Pandavas.Thereafter, he went to fight Bhimsen, where every major warrior of the Pandavas attacked him together, but they were not able to do much harm to him. On the other hand, Dronacharya alone killed thousands of Soma and Srinjaya warriors without breaking a sweat, terrorising the Pandava army. Meanwhile, Iravan, the son of Arjun and the Naga Kanya, was fighting with the Gandharva army of Shakuni. He destroyed their cavalry using his illusionary powers. Seeing this, seven brothers of Shakuni—Gaja, Gavaksha, Vrishabha, Charman, Aarjava, and Shuka—fought against him, but Iravan, taking swords in both hands, cut all seven of them into pieces. On witnessing the horrible deaths of his uncles, Duryodhan went to the Rakshasa king Alambhus and asked him to kill Iravan. Thereafter, on Duryodhan's orders, Alambhus fought Iravan. At first, Iravan destroyed Alambhus's chariot, but the Rakshasa king overpowered him with his demonic powers and cut off his head. On seeing Iravan's death, Ghatotkacha created a terrible roar that struck fear into the hearts of the enemy and went to kill

Duryodhan. He made Duryodhan cover in his own blood. Seeing this, Bhishma, along with other warriors, came to rescue Duryodhan, and they all attacked Ghatotkacha together, but none of them was able to harm him. Thereafter, warriors from the Pandava side came to assist Ghatotkacha and forced the Kuru warriors to flee from the battlefield. On the other hand, Bhimsen fought against Duryodhan, while Neel faced Ashwatthama. Ashwatthama defeated Neel, and Bhimsen defeated Duryodhan, but other warriors, including Dronacharya, came to rescue him. Meanwhile, Ghatotkacha massacred the Kuru army with his demonic powers. To stop him, Bhagadatta arrived on Bhishma's orders, and a fierce battle took place between them, but it ended without a conclusion. Then, other warriors from the Pandava side joined Ghatotkacha against Bhagadatta, but he alone managed to handle all of them. Seeing Bhagadatta fight alone, Dronacharya, along with other warriors, came to support him. While Ghatotkacha fought Bhagadatta, Bhimsen stopped Dronacharya from moving forward, and Abhimanyu defeated Ambhastha. At the same time, Arjun fought against Bhishma and King Susharma. Meanwhile, nine brothers of Duryodhan attacked Bhimsen in front of Dronacharya, and he killed all nine of them with nine arrows. At the same time, Kripacharya and Bhagadatta joined Bhishma against Arjun, but they were not able to defeat him.

Thereafter, a ferocious battle took place between both sides, creating a river of blood. Both sides suffered heavy losses. As a result, Yudhishthir and Bhishma withdrew their armies, ending the eighth day of the war in a draw. On the night of the eighth day, Duryodhan went to Karṇa and requested him to become his commander-in-chief in order to kill the Pandavas. However, Karṇa, being very self-obsessed, refused and put forth a condition that he would only fight if Bhishma gave up fighting. This made Duryodhan very sad. With tears in his eyes, he went to Bhishma and requested him either to kill the Pandavas or give up his weapons so that Karṇa could join the war and ensure their victory. Duryodhan's words struck Bhishma like a whip and saddened him. Under the influence of the Danavas, he took a vow to kill everyone in the Pandava army except Shikhandi, as he had once been a woman, and Bhishma had vowed never to attack anyone who had previously been a woman. This vow made Duryodhan glad, and he ordered his brothers to protect Bhishma from Shikhandi at all costs.

Thereafter, the sun rose and the war began. As promised, Bhishma massacred the Pandava warriors like never before, showing no mercy. Meanwhile, Abhimanyu, along with the five sons of Draupadi, fought a fierce battle against the Rakshasa king Alambhus and ultimately defeated him. On the other hand, Arjun fought against Dronacharya and King Susharma, where he managed to stop Dronacharya.

Therefore, Dronacharya left him and went to fight King Drupad. Seeing Dronacharya leave Arjun, Susharma, along with the Trigarta army, attacked him, but Arjun alone massacred the Trigarta army and defeated King Susharma. On the other hand, Dronacharya defeated Drupad, and Bhimsen defeated King Bahika. Meanwhile, Satyaki tried to stop Bhishma but failed. Therefore, all the warriors from the Pandava side attacked Bhishma together. Seeing this, the Kuru warriors also came to rescue Bhishma. A terrifying battle then broke out between both sides, where Bhishma created mountains of dead bodies from which a stream of blood flowed, turning the battlefield into a literal hell. Seeing this, Shri Krishna's eyes turned red with anger. He jumped from the chariot and ran toward Bhishma, holding his divine chakra in hand. Bhishma welcomed Vasudev to kill him, but Arjun rushed forward and stopped Shri Krishna, assuring him that he would fight the battle with his full strength. Then, both Vasudev and Arjun returned to their chariot and took their places. After that, Bhishma again started killing the Pandava warriors, but soon the sun began to set. Therefore, King Yudhishthir withdrew his army, declaring the Kauravas victorious on the ninth day of the war. At night, the Pandavas secretly went to Bhishma along with Shri Krishna and asked him how to defeat him. Bhishma indirectly told them that he would not attack a woman or a man who had previously been a woman. The Pandavas understood his words and returned to their tent.

The next day, the war resumed. Shikhandi led the Pandava army, while on the other side, the Kuru warriors, on Duryodhan's orders, surrounded Bhishma to protect him. However, under the protection of Arjun and Bhimsen, Shikhandi easily broke through the Kuru formations and reached Bhishma. Knowing Shikhandi's true identity, Bhishma refused to attack him. Shikhandi pierced Bhishma's body with sharp arrows, though Bhishma felt no pain from them. Observing this, Arjun entered into direct combat with Bhishma, and a legendary battle began. Remembering the promise he had made to Vasudev the day before, Arjun first destroyed Bhishma's armour using divine weapons. Then he pierced Bhishma's body with hundreds of arrows, making him appear like a porcupine. He also killed Bhishma's charioteer and horses. Covered with arrows, Bhishma fell to the ground. Seeing him fall, the armies of both sides stopped fighting and gathered around him. On Bhishma's request, Arjun created a bed of arrows to support his body and drew water from the earth to quench his thirst At night, on the tenth day, Karna secretly visited Bhishma. Bhishma praised Karna for his determination to defeat the Pandavas, even though he could not. Then he requested Karna to stay by Duryodhan's side and protect him from the Pandavas, and he blessed him. After that, Karna returned to the camp, where Duryodhan was preparing the strategy for the next day.

ELEVENTH AND TWELFTH DAY

After the defeat of Bhishma, Duryodhan, on Karṇa's advice, appointed Dronacharya as the next commander-in-chief. He then requested Dronacharya to capture Yudhishthir instead of killing him. Dronacharya gladly agreed and assured him that he would capture Yudhishthir. Thereafter, the war began, and Dronacharya directly entered the Pandava formation, killing thousands of Rathis and Maha-Rathis, just like a lion attacking a herd of deer. No warrior from the Pandava side could stop him or even hold him back for a moment, and he finally reached Yudhishthir with the intention of capturing him. At the same time, Arjuna arrived in front of him with great speed, his chariot rumbling and echoing in all directions. He began to surround Dronacharya with a dense shower of arrows. The illustrious Kuntiputra Arjuna placed and released arrows on his bow with such incredible speed that one could not distinguish between the two actions. On that battlefield, Gandivadhari Arjuna created a great darkness with his arrows, and just then, the sun also began to set. Therefore, Dronacharya and Duryodhan withdrew their army. Knowing that the enemies' minds were now distracted from battle and filled with fear, Arjuna also slowly withdrew his forces from the battlefield. At the end of the 11th day, Dronacharya declared that the only way to capture King Yudhishthir was to keep Arjuna away from him. Upon hearing this, Susharma promised Duryodhan that he would engage Arjuna and keep him away. So, at the beginning of the 12th day of the war, King Susharma, along with his brothers and the Trigarta army, challenged Arjuna and lured him away from Yudhishthir. Seeing this, Dronacharya began massacring the Panchal army, killing many Panchala warriors along with the nephews of King Draupad. On the other hand, Bhagadatta's elephants were crushing every chariot and horse that came before them. Many warriors surrounded Bhagadatta to stop him, but none succeeded in halting either him or his elephant. Meanwhile, a tremendous battle took place between Arjuna and the Trigarta army. Arjuna alone killed 10,000 soldiers from the Trigarta army and several thousand from the Narayani Sena, including Susharma's brothers, Satyajit and Sudhanva.Then, on hearing the terrible roar of Bhagadatta's elephant, Arjuna quickly realized that something was wrong. He asked Shri Krishna to steer the chariot toward the direction from which the sound had come. But before they could turn the chariot, Susharma returned and challenged Arjuna once again. Arjuna defeated him and then rushed toward the direction of the terrifying sound.There he saw that Bhagadatta, along with his elephant army, had crushed many of his soldiers and warriors. So Arjuna first killed the elephant army of Bhagadatta. After ,then he confronted him. Thereafter, a fierce battle took place between the two, where

Arjuna had the upper hand. In desperation, Bhagadatta launched the Vaishnavastra at him. Seeing that the Vaishnavastra, released by Bhagadatta, was about to destroy everything, Shri Krishna Himself bore the attack to protect Arjuna. He become Arjuna's shield, bearing the injury on His own chest. As the divine weapon struck Krishna's chest, it transformed into the garland of Vaijayanti — a garland rich with lotus flowers and blossoms of all seasons. Without any panic, Arjuna, now enraged, struck Bhagadatta's elephant with a fierce arrow. The arrow reached the elephant's head like a thunderbolt striking a mountain. It pierced through the elephant's skull with its feathered wings, driving the beast mad and bringing it crashing down to the ground. Then, on Shri Krishna's command, Arjuna pierced Bhagadatta with a powerful arrow, making the Yavana king lifeless. After that, Arjuna entered a berserk state, slaughtering every Kuru Rathi, Maharathi, horse, and elephant in his path, creating a river of blood. Shakuni's twin brothers, Vrishak and Achal, then attacked him together, but Arjuna, without breaking a sweat, beheaded them both with a single arrow. Seeing the severed heads of his brothers fall to the ground, Shakuni's eyes filled with tears. He attacked Arjuna using his delusional powers, but Arjuna countered all of them with divine weapons, forcing him to flee. Meanwhile, King Neel, full of confidence, went directly against Ashwatthama. But Dronaputra, within a moment, cut off his head, terrifying the Pandava army. On another front, Karṇa, along with his brothers and

Nishadraj Brihadrath, surrounded Bhimsen and attacked him with every weapon they had. In a moment, Satyaki and Arjuna arrived to rescue Bhimsen. The three of them then began to decimate Karṇa's army. Karṇa used the Agneyastra against them, but Arjuna countered it with his fierce arrows. Karṇa then rained arrows upon Arjuna, who again countered them and, in front of Karṇa, killed his younger brothers. Thus, in the sight of the Kauravas, Arjuna alone slew the three brothers of Karṇa on that day. Then Bhimasena leapt from his chariot like Garuda and killed fifteen warriors from Karṇa's side with his excellent sword. Dhrishtadyumna slaughter Chandravarma and the Nishadha king Brihatkshatra with his shining sword. After that, Satyaki picked up a second bow and roared like a lion. He wounded Karṇa with sixty-four arrows and then destroyed his bow with two powerful shafts. Seeing Karṇa in danger, Dronacharya, Duryodhan, and Jayadratha rushed in to rescue him — the same Karṇa whom modern writers claim to be unbeatable. Thereafter, the battle resumed, striking terror in the hearts of the cowards. During that chaos, elephant-riders killed elephant-riders, charioteers fought charioteers, horsemen slew horsemen, and infantry warriors clashed with infantry. Chariots crushed elephants, elephant kings trampled great horses, horsemen trampled foot soldiers, and elite charioteers crushed horsemen. Tongues, teeth, and eyes were torn from faces; armours and ornaments lay shattered across the battlefield. In such a state, countless warriors fell to the earth and perished. Both armies were grievously injured, soaked in blood, and stood staring at one another in silent exhaustion. Meanwhile, the sun descended in the west. Then, both sides slowly retreated to their respective camps, ending yet another horrific day of war

THIRTEENTH   DAY

ABHIMANYU' S DEATH

On the 13th day, Dronacharya created an indestructible Chakravyuha filled with mighty warriors. Meanwhile, Susharma, just like the previous day, lured Arjuna away from King Yudhishthir to the southern side of the battlefield. Seeing the unbreakable Chakravyuha formed by Dronacharya, Yudhishthir grew worried. Then, Abhimanyu, easing his concern, declared that he would lead the Pandava army into the Chakravyuha and destroy the Kuru forces. Along with King Yudhishthir, Bhimsen and Satyaki praised and encouraged him to take the lead. On Yudhishthir's command, Abhimanyu marched directly into the Chakravyuha, killing many warriors of the Kuru army. Inside the formation, he rampaged through the Kuru forces, destroying hundreds of Rathis, elephants, and horsemen who came in his path. Seeing Abhimanyu chase away their army, Duryodhan, along with Dronacharya, Kripacharya, Karna, Ashwatthama, Bhurishrava, Brihadbal, Shal, Shalya, and Paurava, began raining arrows on him. But none of them could stop him. On the other hand, Abhimanyu struck each of them with his arrows, severely wounding them and even rendering Shalya unconscious before advancing further. Then Ashmakhaputra tried to stop him, but Abhimanyu killed him, causing chaos within the Kuru ranks. In retaliation, Shalya's brother came forward to avenge him, but he too was slain by Abhimanyu. Witnessing the deaths of Ashmakhaputra and Shalya's brother, Dronacharya's forces retreated from the area where Abhimanyu was fighting.

Furious, Duryodhan sent his brother Dushasan to kill Abhimanyu. But before Dushasan could do anything, Abhimanyu struck him and rendered him unconscious. To protect Dushasan, Karṇa arrived and engaged in a fierce battle with Abhimanyu. Arjuna's son cut down the bows of the warriors with sharp spears tipped with bent ends and tormented Karṇa from all directions. Karṇa responded with numerous arrows, but Abhimanyu endured them fearlessly. Then, within just two moments, the valiant Abhimanyu shot an arrow that cut down Karṇa's bow and his flag, bringing them both to the ground. Karṇa's brother rushed in to help, but Abhimanyu quickly beheaded him in front of Karṇa. Saddened by his brother's death, Karṇa was forced to retreat. Abhimanyu, the son of Subhadra, chased him off the battlefield with arrows tipped with vulture feathers, and then immediately turned to attack other great archers.

At that moment, the fierce and brilliant warrior Abhimanyu, filled with rage, tore through the massive army composed of the four divisions: elephants, cavalry, chariots, and infantry.

कर्णस्तु बहुभिर्बाणैर्धमानोऽभिमन्युना ।
अपायाज्जवनैरश्वैस्ततोऽनीकमभज्यत

Karṇa, who was struck by the numerous arrows shot by Abhimanyu, quickly fled from the battlefield with the help of his swift horses. This caused a stampede in the entire army.
(Drona Parva, AbhimanyuVadha Parva ,chap 41,shloka 8)

Thereafter, Abhimanyu went deeper into the Chakravyuha, killing everything that came in his path. At the same time, Jayadratha—using the power of the boon granted by Bhagwan Shiv—stopped the Pandava army from following Abhimanyu. But this did not affect him; he continued moving forward into the Chakravyuha, slaying thousands of warriors, elephants, horsemen, and charioteers without breaking a sweat. Then, Shalya's sons—Rukmiratha, Vasatiya, and Satyashrava—along with a thousand other kings and princes, attacked him. But Abhimanyu, without fear, faced all of them alone. He killed them all, cutting their bodies into pieces with his arrows and chased the Kuru army like a lion chasing a herd of deer.

Seeing their warriors flee in panic, Dronacharya, Ashwatthama, Brihadbal, Kripacharya, Duryodhan, Karna, Kritavarma, and Shakuni—all filled with rage—attacked the undefeated Abhimanyu. But once again, he repelled them all, forcing them to retreat. Only Lakshmana, the son of Duryodhan, remained to fight him.

A fierce clash followed, during which Lakshmana struck Abhimanyu on the chest with a sharp arrow. In response, Abhimanyu beheaded him with a single arrow. Seeing Lakshmana slain, the warriors around wailed loudly. Duryodhan, devastated by the death of his beloved son, shouted to all the Kshatriyas, "Oh! Kill this Abhimanyu!" Then, six great warriors—Dronacharya, Kripacharya, Karna, Ashwatthama, Brihadbal, and Hridayakumara Kritavarma—surrounded Abhimanyu. But the son of Arjuna wounded them all with sharp arrows and drove them back. Filled with fury, he charged at Jayadratha's vast army with great speed.

At that time, the soldiers of Kalinga, the Nishads, and the valiant sons of Kratha—all clad in armor—tried to block Abhimanyu's path with an elephant force. They launched their best weapons at him, but Abhimanyu defeated them all with his arrows and killed the son of Kratha. Then, he began destroying Jayadratha's army, slaughtering every king and warrior that came before him.

Once again, Dronacharya, Kripacharya, Karṇa, Brihadbal, Ashwatthama, and Kritavarma surrounded him and rained arrows on him from all sides. But Abhimanyu countered them with divine weapons and pierced all the Maharathis with ten arrows each. He destroyed Brihadbal's chariot, flag, and horses and then beheaded him, throwing the Kuru army into chaos.

After slaying Brihadbal, Abhimanyu rode through the battlefield like a lion roaming through the forest. Seeing this, Karṇa pursued him in rage. Then Abhimanyu, the son of Arjuna, shot an arrow that struck Karṇa's ear and followed it with fifty arrows, severely wounding him. Subhadra's son then killed six of Karṇa's valiant ministers, who had fought strange and fierce duels, along with their horses, charioteers, chariots, and flags. In the same way, he slew Ashwaketu, the young son of the King of Magadha, with six arrows, causing him to fall along with his horses and charioteer.

After that, Dussasana's son, Ashwatthama, and Shalya attacked him, but Abhimanyu defeated them all, rendering Shalya unconscious. Seeing this, Gandhara warriors—Shatrunjaya, Chandraketu, Meghavega, Survarcha, and Suryabhasa—all attacked together, but he killed them all and wounded Shakuni severely.

In extreme pain, Shakuni cried out to Duryodhan, "Kill this Abhimanyu together, or else he will kill us all!" At that moment, Karṇa—badly wounded and in great agony from Abhimanyu's arrows—also turned to Dronacharya and said.

आरुजन्नपि मे प्राणान् मोहयन्नपि सायकैः॥ २१॥ प्रहर्षयति मां भूयःसौभद्रःपरवीरहा

Abhimanyu, the destroyer of enemy warriors, although he is causing great pain to my life with his arrows, makes me unconscious.

(Drona Parva, AbhimanyuVadha Parva , chap 48 , shloka 21)

अथ कर्णःपुनर्द्रोणमाहार्जुनिशराहतः॥ २४॥। स्थातव्यमिति तिष्ठामि पीड्यमानोऽभिमन्युना

O teacher! Even though I am being hurt by Abhimanyu's arrows, I am standing here only because a Kshatriya must remain firm on the battlefield (otherwise, I would have run away)

(Drona Parva, AbhimanyuVadha Parva , chap 48 , shloka 24)

Then, Dronacharya laughingly said, "Karṇa! Abhimanyu's armor is impenetrable. This young warrior will soon display his valor. I have told his father the method of wearing the armor. This brave son who will conquer the enemy city certainly knows all the methods (so his armor is impenetrable), but his bow and string can be cut by arrows shot with full concentration. Along with this, the reins of his horses and both the side guards can also be destroyed. O great archer, son of Radha! If you can, then do this. "Hearing this from the Acharya, Karṇa with great haste cut the bow of Abhimanyu who was using weapons with his arrows. Bhojvanshi Kritavarma killed his horses, and Kripacharya killed both the side guards. The remaining Maharathi started showering arrows on Abhimanyu after his bow was cut. Thus, the six ruthless Maharathis who were quick to act on the occasion started showering arrows on a chariotless boy. When his bow was cut and his chariot was destroyed, the illustrious warrior Abhimanyu, obeying his duty, jumped into the sky, holding his shield and sword in his hands. Then Dronacharya and Karṇa destroyed his sword and Shield, making him unarmed. Then, being deprived of his shield and sword, Abhimanyu, his body laden with arrows, again came down from the sky to the earth and, holding his discus in his hand, ran angrily towards Dronacharya. Seeing chakra in his hand, all the kings became very upset, and together, they broke that Chakra into pieces. Then, the great warrior Abhimanyu took a huge mace in his hand. The enemies had deprived him of his bow, chariot, sword and chakra. Therefore, holding the mace in his hand, Abhimanyu attacked Ashwatthama. Seeing that mace raised aloft like a blazing thunderbolt, Ashwatthama, retreated three steps from his chariot seat. Having killed all the four horses and the two side guards of Ashwatthama with that mace, Subhadra's son, with a body full of arrows, began to look like a porcupine. Thereafter, he killed Kalikeya, the son of Subala, and also killed seventy-seven Gandharas who followed him. After this, he killed ten Vasatiya charioteers. After killing seven chariots of Kekayas and ten elephants, he also smashed Dushasan's son chariot along with its horses with the blow of his mace. Then, Dusashan Son, in anger, came after him with a mace. Both those brave warriors, after hitting each other with the front part of the mace on the battlefield, fell on the ground like two downed Indra flags. After that, Dushasana's son first got up and struck the head of Subhadrakumar with his mace. Abhimanyu fell unconscious on the earth, fascinated by the great speed and effort of the mace. In this way, many warriors together killed the lonely Abhimanyu in that battlefield. Thereafter, King Yudhisthir, in sadness, withdrew his army and went back to his camp; therefore, Kaurav also went back to their camp. After the end of the 13th day, when Arjun returns to his camp after defeating Susharma, he finds out about Abhimanyu's death. This news broke him to the core, and somehow, he handled himself. Thereafter, in anger, he takes an oath to kill Jayadratha, the one responsible for the death of his son, before sunset, and if he doesn't fulfil his oath, he will burn himself to ashes. Arjun's oath makes Pandavs both happy and sad at the same time. Thereafter, they went to their respective tents and rested for the night.

FOURTEENTH DAY

On the fourteenth day, Dronacharya once again formed a Chakravyuha to protect Jayadratha from Arjuna. He placed Jayadratha at the center of the formation and surrounded him with mighty warriors like Karṇa, Ashwatthama, and Kripacharya, assigning them the task of guarding him. Dronacharya himself guarded the front of the Chakravyuha. The war began, and Arjuna headed straight toward the Chakravyuha to kill Jayadratha, just like a lion charging toward its prey. Dushasana and Durmukha tried to stop him but failed miserably. After defeating them, Arjuna reached the spot where Dronacharya was guarding the front.Arjuna requested Dronacharya to let him pass, but Dronacharya refused. Arjuna then countered his attacks and forced his way past him, moving deeper into the formation. There, he encountered Kritavarma and rendered him unconscious before advancing further. As he moved deeper into the Chakravyuha, Shrutayudha and Sudakshina, along with their armies, tried to stop him. Arjuna massacred their forces and beheaded both of them. Seeing their brothers killed, Shrutayu and Achyutayu began raining arrows on him. Arjuna stopped their attacks and then cut off both their heads along with their hands. After witnessing the death of their fathers, Niyatayu and Dirghayu attempted to block Arjuna's path, but he killed them as well. Then, soldiers from the Mleccha and Yavana clans surrounded and attacked him. But just as fire burns down a forest, Arjuna burned them all with his arrows, creating a river of blood from the slain Mlecchas and Yavanas. Arjuna moved forward toward Jayadratha. Seeing this, Duryodhana became worried and asked Dronacharya to stop Arjuna, but Dronacharya refused, stating that his duty was to capture King Yudhishthira, not to stop Arjuna. He then gave Duryodhana the divine armour of Mahadev, which Indra had once worn in his battle against Vritrasura. Wearing this divine armour, Duryodhana went to stop Arjuna, but to his misfortune, Arjuna already knew how to counter it, as Devendra had previously taught him the technique. Using that method, Arjuna defeated Duryodhana and advanced deeper into the vyuha toward Jayadratha. Meanwhile, outside the Chakravyuha, a fierce battle took place between the Kuru and Pandava armies, where Ghatotkacha beheaded Rakshasa-raj Alambusha, avenging the death of his cousin Iravan. Seeing Arjuna had gone too far inside the formation, King Yudhishthira became deeply concerned and ordered Satyaki to follow him. Obeying the command, Satyaki passed through Dronacharya and entered the vyuha, where he, like Arjuna, encountered and defeated Kritavarma. He then moved forward to support Arjuna but was blocked by Jalasangha and Trigarta's elephant division. Satyaki killed all the elephants and slew Jalasangha, covering the battlefield with the bodies of the dead beasts. Duryodhana and Kritavarma once again attempted to stop him, but he defeated them too and continued deeper into the vyuha. Seeing this, Dronacharya himself went to fight but could not succeed and was defeated by Satyaki. Thereafter, Satyaki moved forward toward Arjuna, cutting the Kuru army into pieces with his arrows. This made King Sudarshan very angry, and he came to duel with him, but Satyaki cut off his head with a single arrow. Then, the Yavana and Kamboja soldiers tried to stop him, but he burned them all with his fiery arrows and advanced further. Dushasana stopped him with an army of Mlecchas, who were highly skilled in fighting with stones and started raining stones on him. Satyaki countered the attack with divine weapons and massacred the Mlecchas, forcing Dushasana to flee, and continued toward Arjuna. Meanwhile, on the other side, King Yudhishthira, having received no sign of either Satyaki or Arjuna, grew worried and sent Bhimsen into the Chakravyuha. Just like the others, Bhimsen faced Dronacharya, but this time, Dronacharya did not let him pass. This enraged Bhimsen, and he jumped off his chariot. He threw Dronacharya along with his chariot into the air, but Dronacharya landed on another chariot, which Bhimsen again hurled into the air, destroying it. Bhimsen did this four to five times, and finally, seeing his fury, Dronacharya allowed him to pass. Like Arjuna and Satyaki, Bhimsen confronted Kritavarma and defeated him. Then, eleven Kauravas surrounded him, but remembering his enmity with them, he killed all eleven with eleven arrows. After that, Anu and Vinda tried to stop him, but Bhimsen cut off their heads with a single arrow. He then moved deeper into the

Chakravyuha, killing everyone who came in his path—be it horsemen, soldiers, elephants, or warriors. At last, upon reaching near Arjuna and Satyaki, he blew his conch shell loudly, sending a signal to King Yudhishthira that all three of them were safe.

Bhimsen vs Karṇa

Thereafter, seeing Bhimsen killing the Kaurava brothers, Karṇa went after him like a wild boar, and Bhimsen faced him with his fierce arrows. A massive battle then broke out between them, with both warriors raining arrows on each other. In a fit of rage, Bhimsen cut off Karṇa's bow, leaving him empty-handed. Karṇa then picked up another bow, strung it quickly, and wounded Bhimsen on the battlefield. Bhimsen retaliated and pierced Karṇa with several sharp arrows, causing streams of blood to pour from his chest as if ochre metal (geru) was flowing from a mountain. Karṇa became greatly disturbed after being struck by such a deep blow. In response, he pulled his bowstring to his ear and pierced Bhimsen with numerous arrows, then followed up with hundreds and thousands more. Suffering under the relentless attack of the powerful archer Karṇa, Bhimsen swiftly cut the string of Karṇa's bow with a razor-headed arrow, then beheaded his charioteer and killed his horses. Left without support, Karṇa fled the battlefield on another chariot.

हताश्वात् तु रथात् कर्णः समाप्लुत्य विशाम्पते । स्यन्दनं वृषसेनस्य तूर्णमापुप्लुवे भयात् ॥

At that time, Karṇa, in fear, jumped from that horseless chariot and immediately sat on Vrishasena's chariot.

(Dronaparva,JayadrathaVadha parva,chap 129,shlok 33)

After defeating Karṇa on the battlefield, the strong and glorious Bhimasena let out a lion's roar, his voice as deep as the thunder of clouds. Hearing Bhima's great roar, King Yudhishthira felt immense joy, knowing that Karṇa had been defeated by him in battle. At that moment, the Pandava army heard the sound of conch shells all around. In response, the Kuru soldiers began roaring upon hearing the enemy's conches, trying to instill fear in their hearts. Then, Karṇa challenged Bhimasena to another duel, which he accepted. A fierce and terrifying battle followed, where both warriors pierced each other with deadly arrows, drenching themselves in blood. As before, Bhima destroyed Karṇa's bow and killed his horses, forcing Karṇa to mount another chariot to continue the fight. Bhima, remembering Karṇa's harsh words during the gambling match, again destroyed his chariot and horses, leaving Karṇa anxious and unsure of what to do next. Just then, Durmarshana came to his rescue, but Bhima killed him with a single arrow, remembering his vow to slay all 100 Kauravas. Seizing the moment, Karṇa returned with a new chariot and brought along eleven of Duryodhana's brothers. Another intense battle began, during which

Bhima cut down Karṇa's bow eleven times and, each time, killed one of Duryodhana's brothers—thus slaying all eleven and leaving Karṇa defenseless. In the end, Bhima destroyed Karṇa's chariot, forcing him to flee once more. Tears welled in Karṇa's eyes as he mourned the death of Duryodhana's brothers, but he soon returned on yet another chariot and unleashed a heavy shower of arrows upon Bhimasena. Bhima responded with an equally fierce counterattack, and the battlefield became completely covered with arrows, killing everything in their surroundings. Seven more of Duryodhana's brothers arrived to support Karṇa, but Bhima killed all seven with seven arrows in front of him. Witnessing this, Karṇa was devastated and enraged, which only intensified their deadly duel. In his fury, Bhima cut off Karṇa's golden earring, causing a deep wound in his ear, and then pierced his chest with deadly arrows, rendering him unconscious for a brief time. Upon regaining consciousness, Karṇa once again showered Bhima with arrows, which Bhima countered with his own. Both warriors pierced each other's bodies with sharp arrows until Bhima let out a fierce roar and cut down the bow of Sutaputra with a razor-headed arrow. Karṇa threw away the broken bow and picked up another, swift and light, but Bhima cut it in half almost instantly. In the same way, Bhima destroyed Karṇa's third, fourth, fifth, sixth, seventh, eighth, ninth, tenth, eleventh, twelfth, thirteenth, fourteenth, fifteenth, and sixteenth bows, one after another. Not only that, Bhimasena swiftly cut off Karṇa's seventeenth, eighteenth, and many more bows, leaving him completely defenseless. Seeing Karṇa repeatedly defeated by Bhimasena, Narakasura took full control of Karṇa's body, transforming his expression from worry to a creepy and terrifying look. Karṇa (possessed by Narakasura) then covered Bhimasena with a storm of arrows, terrifying everyone except Bhimasena. Bhima responded with divine weapons, but Karṇa (under Narakasura's control) destroyed his chariot, leaving him momentarily vulnerable. After this, Narakasura returned control of the body to Karṇa. Bhimasena, using the body of a dead elephant as cover, somehow reached near Karṇa's chariot and began hurling elephant carcasses at him. As Karṇa cut them down, Bhimasena seized the chariot and held it down. Seeing him so close, Karṇa hid at the rear of the chariot. Bhimasena prepared his fist to kill him, but remembering Arjuna's vow to slay Karṇa, he restrained himself and turned away, heading toward where Arjuna was fighting. Meanwhile, the human Alambusha and Dushasana blocked Satyaki's path, leading to a fierce battle. Satyaki destroyed Dushasana's chariot, and upon reaching Alambusha, he beheaded him with his sword and then moved forward toward Arjuna.

Bhurishrava's death

As Satyaki reached near Arjuna, Bhurishrava stopped him from advancing, and an intense duel took place between them. Both warriors destroyed each other's chariots and killed each other's charioteers and horses. Thereafter, they began fighting with swords. For a moment, their duel became so fierce that it was difficult to predict its outcome. Soon after, Bhurishrava overpowered Satyaki, threw him to the ground, and placed his foot on Satyaki's chest. Seeing that Satyaki was on the verge of death, Arjuna intervened and cut off Bhurishrava's hand—the one holding the sword. With his hand severed, Bhurishrava decided to undertake a fast unto death. He prepared a seat of arrows, sat upon it, and began his fast. Then, Satyaki, seizing the opportunity, cut off Bhurishrava's head, demoralizing the Kuru army

Jayadratha 's death

After helping Satyaki, Arjuna began to move toward Jayadratha, who was being guarded by Karṇa, Ashwatthama, Kripacharya, Duryodhana, Shalya, and Shakuni. Seeing Arjuna approaching, Duryodhana urged Karṇa to stop him at any cost. Following Duryodhana's order, Karṇa engaged Arjuna in battle and covered him with a thousand arrows. This enraged Arjuna, and with just five arrows, he killed Karṇa's four horses and charioteer, rendering his chariot useless. He then covered Karṇa with a volley of arrows. As Karṇa became disoriented in the rain of arrows, Ashwatthama came to his aid and took him away from the battlefield to save his life. Arjuna then advanced toward Jayadratha, who was still protected by the six great warriors. All of them tried to stop him, but Arjuna filled the entire battlefield with arrows, slaying everything that came in his path. He created a mountain of severed human heads, causing even the bravest warriors to lose hope, though they still made every effort to protect Jayadratha. Seeing that the sun was about to set, Shree Krishna cleverly covered the sky with dark clouds. Believing that the sun had set, Jayadratha came out from behind the protection of the Maharathis and confidently challenged Arjuna. At that moment, Vasudeva cleared the sky. Filled with rage, Arjuna destroyed Jayadratha's chariot along with his horses and charioteer, wounding him severely. Then, on Shree Krishna's advice, Arjuna beheaded Jayadratha and sent his head flying to a forest where his father was performing penance. Jayadratha's head landed in his father's lap, disturbing his meditation. In shock, his father threw the head to the ground, and as it touched the earth, his own head burst into pieces, thus fulfilling his boon. Enraged by Jayadratha's death, Kripacharya and Ashwatthama launched a combined attack on Arjuna, but without showing any sign of fatigue, Arjuna countered their assault and wounded them badly, even rendering Kripacharya unconscious. Thereafter, as he proceeded toward Satyaki, Karna and Dushasana tried to stop him. Satyaki intervened in the battle and defeated both Karna and Dushasana, forcing them to flee. Finally, Arjuna, Shree Krishna, and Satyaki united with Bhimasena, and all of them together blew their conch shells in triumph On hearing the sound of the conch shells, King Yudhishthira understood that Jayadratha had been killed, and he felt great relief upon learning this. Thereafter, Arjuna, Bhimasena, and Satyaki returned to him, and he praised all three for the immense valour they had shown in that day's battle by accomplishing a task that even the Devas would have found impossible. Meanwhile, Duryodhana was deeply upset over Jayadratha's death and, in frustration, spoke harshly to Dronacharya. Enraged and under the influence of Asuric forces, Dronacharya decided to violate the rules of war by continuing the battle into the night. He then launched a fierce attack on the Pandava army. The Pandavas responded to Dronacharya's assault, and at first, Duryodhana wreaked havoc on the Panchala forces, killing many warriors with his arrows. But soon, Bhimasena arrived and defeated Duryodhana, saving the Panchala army from his fury. Dronacharya then came to Duryodhana's aid and began scorching the Panchala army with a storm of arrows. He also killed the son of King Drupada and the brother of King Virata, spreading fear throughout the Pandava ranks. Meanwhile, Bhimasena and Satyaki engaged in a fierce battle with the father-son duo, Bahika and Somadatta. Bhimasena crushed the head of King Bahika with his mace, while Satyaki cut off Somadatta's head with an arrow, bringing an end to the Bahika dynasty.

Ghatochkach death

Meanwhile, a frightening battle took place between Ghatotkacha's rakshasa army and Ashwatthama, where he alone destroyed the entire rakshasa army and killed Ghatotkacha's son, Anjanaparva. This made Ghatotkacha extremely angry; therefore, he started raining arrows on him. Ashwatthama responded by raining arrows in return. After that, Ashwatthama destroyed his chariot using divine weapons. Then, Ghatotkacha struck him from all directions with every type of weapon, leaving him severely wounded. Seeing Ashwatthama fighting alone against Ghatotkacha, Karṇa and others came to assist him, but they too were soon wounded by the demonic powers of Ghatotkacha. Thereafter, Narakasura, witnessing Ghatotkacha's immense power, took control of Karṇa's body. Then, an intense duel began, in which Karṇa (possessed by Narakasura) destroyed all the illusions created by Ghatotkacha. Ghatotkacha then started hurling stones at Karṇa (Narakasura), but Karṇa countered them with divine weapons. Again, Ghatotkacha launched a rain of different weapons, destroying Karṇa's chariot and leaving him chariotless. Seeing no other option to stop him, Karṇa finally decided to use the Amogha Shakti, which he had reserved for Arjuna, and fired it at Ghatotkacha. The Amogha Shakti tore through Ghatotkacha's chest, making him fall to the ground.But before dying, Ghatotkacha expanded his body to a massive size and collapsed on Duryodhana's Akshauhini army, crushing and killing the entire force. Seeing Ghatotkacha dead, the Pandavas became deeply saddened and withdrew their army to allow them rest, as they had fought all night. However, Duryodhana, enraged by Jayadratha's death, ordered Dronacharya to attack the resting army of Yudhishthira. But Dronacharya refused to obey the order and, like Yudhishthira, allowed the Kuru army to rest for a while

Dronacharya's death

The next day, the war began again. Dronacharya, remembering the toxic words of Duryodhana and being under the control of an Asura, rampaged through the Pandava army, killing ten thousand soldiers at a time using divine weapons. He then killed King Drupada and King Virata with just two arrows, which made Dhrishtadyumna's eyes red with anger. However, even with great effort, he could not defeat Dronacharya. Seeing this, Shree Krishna asked Bhimsen to kill an elephant named Ashwatthama and then instructed King Yudhishthira to lie about Ashwatthama's death, as he had never lied in his life. Following Shree Krishna's words, Bhimsen killed the elephant named Ashwatthama and shouted that Ashwatthama had died. But Dronacharya did not believe him and continued fighting.Then Yudhishthira shouted, "Ashwatthama is dead," and in a lower voice added, "The one who died is not your guru's son, but an elephant." Since Dronacharya knew that King Yudhishthira never lied, he believed his words and went into deep shock. Seizing the opportunity, Dhrishtadyumna jumped onto his chariot, grabbed his head, cut it off with his sword, and threw it toward the Kuru army, creating great chaos among them. Upon hearing the news of the death of Acharya Drona of the golden chariot, Duryodhana became distressed and, in great fear, ran away from the battlefield along with his charioteers. Karṇa also fled in fear, followed by his massive army. The rest of the warriors fled as well. Seeing them running, Ashwatthama stopped them and asked what had happened, but no one spoke a word. Then Kripacharya stepped forward and informed him about Dronacharya's death.Upon hearing this, Ashwatthama became extremely angry. Under the influence of an Asura, he launched the Narayana Astra at the Pandavas. But following Shree Krishna's advice, the Pandavas surrendered themselves to the Narayana Astra and saved their lives. Seeing his Narayana Astra fail, Ashwatthama then launched the Agneya Astra, but Shree Krishna and Arjuna absorbed it within themselves, protecting the Pandava army. Realizing that both his astras had failed, Ashwatthama lost all hope and sadly returned to the camp along with the Kuru army, thus ending the fifteenth day of the war

THE FINAL BATTLE

After the death of Dronacharya, Duryodhana, on Ashwatthama's advice, appointed Karṇa as the next commander-in-chief of the Kuru army. Thereafter, the battle resumed, and Bhimasena, displaying great valour, killed Kshemadurthi, causing the Kuru army to flee in fear. Seeing his soldiers retreating from Bhimasena, Ashwatthama arrived to confront him, and in their fierce duel, both warriors rendered each other unconscious. Meanwhile, Arjuna nearly annihilated the Trigarta army, killing Susharma's brothers and their sons. After regaining consciousness, Ashwatthama attacked King Paundya and beheaded him, spreading terror among the Dravida forces. Arjuna then engaged Ashwatthama in battle and defeated him by wounding him severely. At the same time, Kripacharya and Karṇa began slaughtering the Panchala soldiers. Shikhandi and Nakula attempted to stop them but were defeated by Karṇa and Kripacharya. On another front, a duel took place between Yudhishthira and Duryodhana, where Yudhishthira emerged victorious. Spotting Karṇa on the battlefield, Yudhishthira attacked him, showering him with arrows and leaving him heavily wounded. After this, the chief warriors of the Pandava army launched a collective assault on Karṇa. Yudhamanyu, Shikhandi, the five sons of Draupadi, the Prabhadrakas, Uttamauja, Yuyutsu, Nakula and Sahadeva, Dhrishtadyumna, and the armies of Chedi, Karusha, Matsya, and Kekaya, along with mighty warriors like Chekitana and Dhar—all attacked Karṇa. Charioteers, horsemen, elephant riders, and foot soldiers displayed terrifying valour and surrounded Karṇa from all sides, raining a variety of weapons upon him while uttering dreadful threats. But like a powerful wind that uproots trees, Karṇa shattered their weapon storm with his sharp arrows and repelled them with the sheer force of his archery. Consumed with rage, he destroyed charioteers, elephants with their mahouts, horses with riders, and countless foot soldiers. The Pandava army, crushed under the might of Karṇa's weapons, was stripped of its weapons, vehicles, and lives, and many fled the battlefield in terror. Then Arjuna, smiling, countered Karṇa's attack, destroying his weapons and filling the sky, sun, and earth with a shower of arrows. Struck by Arjuna's onslaught, the Kaurava army—comprising infantry, cavalry, chariots, and elephants—scattered in panic, running in circles to save their lives. As the soldiers were being hit by arrows and overwhelmed by fear and pain, they fled in all directions. While the victorious soldiers continued their assault, the sun eventually reached the horizon and set. With nightfall approaching, both armies withdrew to their respective camps

Karṇa's death

Seeing Karṇa defeated once again, Narakasura finally took full control over his body and lifted the Vijaya Dhanush of Bhagwan Rudra, which had been given by Sage Parashurama and which Karṇa himself could never properly control. Thereafter, he demanded King Shalya as his charioteer, as Shalya was the only one capable of controlling horses with the same skill as Shree Krishna. On Karṇa's (Narakasura's) request, Duryodhana asked Shalya to become his charioteer. Though Shalya initially refused, he eventually agreed after Duryodhana praised him and compared him to Shree Krishna. With this, preparations for the final battle began, and both armies stood face to face. During the battle, King Shalya tried to demoralize Karṇa by constantly praising Arjuna and Shree Krishna. In response, Karṇa (Narakasura) acknowledged the power of Shree Krishna, and Arjuna reminded him of the curses that were destined to affect him.

First Curse:

"It is a story of the past, with the desire to obtain divine weapons. I used to live with Parashurama in the guise of a Brahmin. O Shalya! There was also Devraj Indra, who wanted the welfare of Arjuna and created obstacles in my work. One day, Gurudev slept with his head on my thigh. At that time, Indra entered the hideous body of an insect and came near my thigh and bit it, causing a huge wound in it and by doing this, he created obstacles in my desire. Due to the wound in my thigh, a huge amount of thick blood started flowing from my thigh, but I was not at all disturbed for fear of waking up. Then, when Guruji woke up, he saw something like this. Shalya! Seeing me so patient, he said- 'Oh! You are not a Brahmin; then who are you? Tell me the truth. ' Then I gave him my true introduction and said- 'Lord! I am a Sut'. Thereafter, after hearing my story, the great ascetic Parshuram Ji became very angry with me. He cursed me and said- 'Suta! You have obtained this Brahmastra by deceit. Therefore, when you need it, you will not remember this weapon. ".

(Note: Parshuram cursed him for lying, not for belonging to suta varna because in Shastra, it's a great sin to deceit a Guru.)

2nd Curse

 "Once upon a time, I was roaming around the ashram of a Brahmin named Vijay to practice weapons. At that time, while shooting a fierce and dangerous arrow, I unknowingly, due to carelessness, killed the calf of that Brahmin's cow. Shalya! Then that Brahmin came to me while roaming in solitude and said, 'You have killed the calf of my Homa Dhenuk due to negligence. Therefore, at the time when you are fighting in the battlefield and are extremely frightened, the wheel of your chariot should fall into the pit. O King of Madra, Shalya, was giving one thousand hundred and six hundred bulls to the Brahmin but could not receive his blessings. Even after giving me seven hundred elephants with teeth like ploughshares and hundreds of slaves and maids, that great Brahmin did not show mercy on me. I started offering all the wealth I had, a prosperous house full of all pleasures, to that Brahmin with great respect, but he did not wish to take anything. At that time, I tried to apologise for my crime. Then the Brahmin said- 'Sut! Whatever I have said will happen. That moment cannot be changed. After saying this, the Brahmin went away in a different direction". (Note: Karṇa had tried to compare a calf who is just like a family member to Brahmin with money.)

 After telling him about his curse, Karṇa (Naraksura) again started insulting women of his country by calling them prostitutes, and then King Shalya replied to him, "Karṇa! What happens in the country of Ang where you have been made the king? When relatives fall ill, they are abandoned. People there sell their wives and children in the open market. Know your faults and become calm and free from anger as per what Bhishma told you that day while counting the charioteers and super-charioteers. Karṇa! Everywhere, there are Brahmins. Everywhere, there are Kshatriyas, Vaishyas and Shudras, and in all countries, there are pious women who follow the best vows. In all countries, there live kings who follow their dharma, who suppress the wicked and righteous people who reside everywhere.

Karṇa! Just because people live in a country, they do not commit sins. In that country, people become such great men due to their good character and nature that even gods cannot match them. "Then King Duryodhana stopped both Karṇa and Shalya. He persuaded Karṇa(Naraksura) to refuse in a friendly manner and stopped Shalya with folded hands. Karṇa(Naraksura) did not reply to Duryodhan's refusal, and Shalya also turned towards the enemies. Then Karṇa(Naraksura) smiled and ordered Shalya to move ahead and said," Let's go, let's go". Thereafter, the war began on one side. Arjun went inside Susharm's army, and Karṇa (Narakasur) went into the Dravida & Panchal army, destroying it. Then Drishtadymna, Shikhandi, Shrutakarma, and the five sons of Draupadi together came to kill Karṇa. But they all miserably failed & got defeated by Karṇa(Narakasur). Thereafter, Yudhisthir came there to fight him, then Karṇa(Narakasura) started showering arrows on him, making him wounded, seeing Bhimsen come to rescue him. Then a terrible battle happened between them. Bhimasena attacked Karṇa in just two moments. Seeing him coming towards him, Karṇa (Narakasur), filled with rage, attacked him in the chest with a bow and arrow. Then, that brave man endowed with immense self-confidence covered him with a shower of his arrows. When Suta's son wounded him, he also covered him with arrows and pierced Karṇa(Naraksura) with nine sharp arrows having a bent knot. Then, Karṇa shot several arrows and broke Bhimasen's bow into two pieces. When his bow was cut, he inflicted a deep wound on his chest with a very sharp arrow that pierced all the coverings. Bhimasena, the penetrative, took up his second bow and struck the vital spots of the son of a charioteer with sharp arrows and roared as if shaking the earth and the sky. Then, due to his entire body being injured by Karṇa's arrows, Pandu's son Bhimsen became unconscious with anger. His eyes turned red with anger and jealousy. With the desire to kill Suta's son, he prepared an arrow on his bow that was extremely fast, capable of carrying a load, excellent and capable of shattering mountains. That arrow, which was released from the hand of the powerful Bhimasena and made a sound like thunderbolt and lightning, pierced Karṇa on the battlefield as if the force of the thunderbolt had pierced the mountain. After receiving a severe blow from Bhimasena, the commander, Sutaputra Karṇa, fell unconscious and sat down in the chariot seat. His whole body got soaked in blood. That brave man who had suppressed his enemies had become lifeless. Thereafter, Madraraj, seeing Suta's son Karṇa unconscious, ran away from the battlefield in a chariot. After gaining conscious Narakasura inside, Karṇa made a frightening sound, challenging Bhimsen and creating fear among the Pandav's army.Listening to this, Bhimsen quickly went toward Karn(Narakasura) to fight him. Thereafter, a bloody duel started between them, where six brothers of Duryodhan also came to help Karṇa. But Bhimsen killed them, making Karṇa(Narakasura) even more angry. Then Karṇa first wounded Bhimsen with three arrows, after which he killed his sarthi along with the horses, making his Chariot useless. Being chariotless, the powerful Bhimasena, laughingly jumped from that excellent chariot, holding his mace in his hand. Just as the wind quickly blows away the autumn clouds, similarly, Bhimasena, jumping with great force, began destroying the Kaurava army with the blows of his mace. Bhimasena, the tormentor of enemies, suddenly killed seven hundred elephants, skilled in attacking and having teeth like the rod of a spear, in anger. Thus, Nakul and Sahadev came there to rescue him, but Karṇa(Narakasur) defeated them both and made them flee from there, along with Bhimsen. On the other hand, Ashwatthama, seeing Arjun massacring Susharma's army, went there to fight him. Thereafter, Arjun defeats him but spares his life, considering him to be his Teacher's son. On the other hand, Satyaki, who had defeated Karṇa in previous battle struggles against him, therefore observed this King Yudhishtir came to their to help, but Karṇa(Narakasura) wounded him so badly with his deadly . King Yudhisthir had to run away from there to his camp to heal himself. Arjun, on returning to meet King Yudhisthir, gets to know this from Bhimsen. Then, giving responsibility of war to Bhimsen, he went to see King Yudhisthir in his camp. Where on the camp, he and Shree Krishna made Yudhisthir ensures that today will be the last day of Karṇa. Thereafter, Arjun again takes an oath to kill Karṇa today or get killed by him. This made Yudhisthir very happy, and then he blessed him to win and made him return to the war. On the way between the battlefield and the camp, Arjun became a little worried about the sudden change in Karṇa 's behaviour. Then Shree Krishna motivates him by making him remember the atrocities of both Karṇa and Duryodhan and orders him to kill Karṇa, ending this war once and for all. Thus, Arjun leaves his tension and prepares himself for the final battle against Vikartan Karṇa. On reaching the battlefield, he met Bhimsen, and then they went towards Karṇa, destroying everything that came in their way with their arrows, creating whole ponds of Human blood filled with the hands, legs and heads of warriors. On the other hand, Karṇa(Narakasur) also came toward Arjun, massacring enemies in his way. Thereafter Shakuni tries to stop them but defeating him Bhimsen went toward forward along with Arjun later Satyaki also joined them. As they move forward toward Karṇa Dushan and Karṇa 's son, Prasein stopped Bhimsen and Satyaki. After then Satyaki behaded Prasein and on the hand Bhimsen remembering Draupadi's Vastra haran destroys Dussashan's Chariots. After destroying his chariot, Bhimsen himself went on the ground and started wrestling with him. Thereafter, Climbing on Dushasan's chest, Bhimasena held him forcefully with both hands and, roaring, he said to all the warriors- 'Today, Dushasan's arm is being torn off. He now wants to give up his life. Whoever has strength, come and save him from my hands. ' enraged Bhimasena tore off Dushasan's arm with force with just one hand. Bhimasena started beating him with that arm in front of all the warriors. After this,he tore open the chest of Dushasan lying on the ground and started trying to drink his hot blood.and started drinking his hot blood with great pleasure. Seeing him killing and drinking Dushasan 's blood, Kuru soldiers get very terrified and run toward Karṇa to save themselves. Thus, seeing their brother dead, Duryodhan's 10 brothers together attacked him, but Bhimsen, with only 10 arrows, killed them all. Meanwhile, seeing that all the armies, the horses of Nakul being killed by Vrishasena and Shree Krishna being injured, attacked Vrishasena on the battlefield. At that time, Vrishasena was standing in front of Karṇa. Then, the great warrior Vrishasena, son of Karṇa, immediately injured Arjuna, son of Kunti, with a sharp arrow on the battlefield and started roaring. After this, Vrishasena again attacked Arjuna's left arm with fierce arrows, and after wounding Shri Krishna with nine arrows, he again wounded Kunti's son Arjuna with ten arrows. Thereafter, the crown-wearing Mahatma Arjun, having firmly resolved to kill Karṇa's son on the battlefield, angrily crooked his forehead eyebrows at three places and quickly began shooting arrows at the mouth of the battlefield. Then Arjuna, wearing a crown, smilingly attacked him fearlessly with ten arrows on his vital spots. Then, with four sharp knives, he cut off his bow, both his arms and his head. Being wounded by Arjun's arrows, Vrishasena lost his arms and head and fell from the chariot on the ground. The swift-acting charioteer's son Karṇa(Naraksura), seeing his son struck by an arrow and falling from the chariot, became agitated at the death of his son and filled with anger. He drove his chariot at great speed towards Arjuna's chariot. Thereafter, Shree Krishna told Arjuna that Karṇa was coming toward them. Then Arjun confidently replied that no matter what happened, he would going to kill Karṇa today, making Duryodhan helpless, and asked him to go toward Karṇa as time was running out. When Arjuna said this, Lord Krishna honored him by blessing him with victory and at that time, the horses, which were as fast as mind, moved forward at great speed. That Manojava chariot of Pandu's son Arjuna in a moment stood in front of Karṇa's chariot.

The Final Duel

When Karṇa saw Vrishasena killed, he was overcome with grief and anger and started shedding tears from his eyes for the loss of his son. Then Karṇa (Narakasur), with his eyes turning red with anger, came in front of his enemy Dhananjaya on a chariot, challenging him for battle. When those two chariots, covered with tiger skin and shining like the sun, came together, the people there saw them as if two suns had risen. Seeing those two chariots standing next to each other, all the kings started roaring and praising each other profusely.Soldiers standing there started clapping their arms and waving their clothes. Thereafter, to increase the joy of Karṇa, the Kaurava soldiers started playing musical instruments and blowing conches all around there. In the same way, all the Pandavas also started encouraging Arjuna and started echoing in all directions the sound of musical instruments and conches.

At the the same time Devtas, Asuras, Yakshas, marutas, Rishis along with Bhagwan Shiva and Bhagwan Brahma gathered there in the sky . Where Asura, Yatudhaan, Rakshas, Pishach and Guhyak Ghosts, vampires, all of them sided with Karṇa. On the other hand sages, the Devatas except Bhagwan Aditya, the Siddhas, Garuda, the birds, , the Upavedas, the Upanishads, , the collections and the entire Vedas including the Itihasa-Puranas, Vasuki, Chitrasen, Takshak Manik, the entire serpent group, – all of them became in favor of Arjuna. Then an argument started between Indra and Surya dev about their therefore seeing that whole group getting divded into two sides where Devta on Arjun's side and Asura on Karṇa's side. Then Indra asked both Bhagwan Brahma & Mahadev who was going to win this duel. Then, both of them said, "Mahatma Arjun's victory is certain. Indra! This Savyasachi Arjun satisfied Agnidev in the Khandav forest and went to heaven and helped you as well. 'Karṇa is a man of demon-wing; Therefore, he should be defeated - by doing so, the work of the devtas will be accomplished. Deveshwar! One's work is more important than everyone else's.Mahatma Arjun is always ready for truth and dharma; Therefore, they will win, there is no doubt about it. This world cannot survive if Shri Krishna and Arjun are angry; Only the great men Shri Krishna and Arjun continuously create the world. No one in the world of gods or the world of humans can compare these two. Along with the gods, sages and bards, the three worlds, all the gods, and all the ghosts are under their control. Due to their influence, the entire world is engaged in its actions. Let the valiant and brave Karṇa attain the best of the worlds, but victory must surely be of Sri Krishna and Arjuna. "

On the other hand, Ashwatthama, observing the signs from both sides, told Duryodhan that the signs he was seeing indicated that Arjun will going to win this duel, killing Karṇa, so the best thing he could do now was to have a treaty with Pandavs. But Duryodhan calmly refused his offer for peace, saying that both had given each other irreversible damage, whose only solution is the win of one side and the defeat of the other side. Thereafter, all the warriors of the Kaurava and Pandava sides, filled with great joy, started killing all the enemies, making the battlefield and all directions echo with musical instruments, conch sound, roar of lions and noise. Then a huge battle happened between both the filling the air full of arrows thereafter, when the soldiers of both side could not see anything in the darkness caused by the arrows, they became frightened and took refuge under the two chief charioteers. Then a wonderful battle started all around. Then, Karṇa(Narakasur) and Arjun moved towards each other for war. Just as a great cloud is ready to clash with another cloud or as a mountain is ready to clash with another mountain by the will of God, in the same way, both the heroes came face to face, showering arrows accompanied by the deep sound of bowstrings, palms and wheels of the chariot. Just as two large lakes, which were full of lotuses, water lilies, fishes and tortoises and covered with flocks of birds, come together when driven by the wind, in the same way, their two chariots, decorated with flags, collided with each other. Both of them were as brave as Indra and as skilled as him. Like Indra and Vritrasur, they started hurting each other with Indra's thunderbolt-like arrows. Thereafter, warriors from both sides started praising their respective warriors. Thereafter, Karṇa(Narakasur) first pierced Arjuna with ten huge arrows, then Arjuna too smilingly pierced Karṇa's armpit with ten sharp arrows. In that war, both Karṇa(Narakasur), and Arjuna, filled with extreme anger, began to pierce each other with beautiful feathered arrows. They were harming each other and attacking each other with their noses. Arjuna used to attack Karṇa(Narakasur) with arrows while looking sarcastically with his eyebrows, but all those arrows shot by Arjuna, son of Pandu, were soon destroyed by Karṇa(Narakasur). Then Indrakumar Arjun used the enemy-killing firearm on Karṇa. The form of that firearm spread across the earth, sky, direction and the path of the sun and ignited there, burning everything around it. Therefore, Karṇa(Narakasur) encountered it with Varun Astra ending intensity of Agnyastra.Then clouds gathered with great speed and covered all directions with darkness. The last part of the directions started appearing like a black mountain. The clouds had flooded the entire area with water. Surrounded by clouds, all directions became covered with darkness; Therefore, nothing was visible. Thereafter, after disintegrating all the cloud groups coming from Karna(Narakasur) with his Vayvayastra, Arjuna, invincible to the enemies, summoned the Gandiva bow, its string and arrows and manifested the most effective Vajrastra, which was the favorite weapon of Lord Indra. Then thousands of Sharp arrows came from that Astra, piercing the whole body of Karna and giving him tremendous pain.Karna (Narakasur) manifested Bhargavastra and cut the arrows into pieces that appeared from Arjuna's Vajrastra, and by suppressing his weapons with his weapon, he destroyed the chariots, elephants and foot soldiers in the battlefield. Thereafter, they both showed tremendous valour and started killing each army, making the battlefield full of soldiers' body parts. Then Arjun laughingly wounded Shalya with ten arrows and shattered his armour. Then he wounded Karna(Narakasur) with twelve well-shot arrows and again pierced him with seven arrows. Then, Karna's entire body got torn apart after being deeply wounded by the fierce arrows shot from Arjuna's bow. He was bathed in blood. Then Arjun laughingly wounded Shalya with ten arrows and shattered his armour. Then he wounded Karna(Narakasur) with twelve well-shot arrows and again pierced him with seven arrows. Then, Karna's entire body was torn apart after being deeply wounded by the fierce arrows shot from Arjuna's bow.

He was bathed in blood. Then, in response, Karṇa(Narakasur) release snake arrows on both Shree Krishna and Arjun, wounding them badly. Therefore, Arjun, in immense anger, flung flaming arrows at him, inflicting deep wounds on his vital organs. Although Karṇa became very sad about his condition, with the power of Narakasur, he stood there, firmly showing no fear. Thereafter, Arjun, filled with anger, spread such a net of arrows that the directions, the directions, the sun's light and Karṇa's chariot all became invisible like the sky covered with fog. Arjun sent Karṇa's wheel protector, foot protector, forward and back protector, all the main heroes of the Kaurava group, who were always ready for the war as per the orders of Duryodhana and whose number was two thousand, in a single moment sent them into the cheeks of Kaal along with the chariots, horses and charioteers. Making them flee from the battlefield, even Duryodhan, couldn't be able to stop them from running away. In that great duel, Arjuna used every weapon with full force to kill Karṇa in anger, but Karṇa(Narakasur) used his fierce arrows to cut them in the sky itself. In this way, while fighting on the battlefield, among the two heroes, in terms of bravery, weapon handling, might, and effort, sometimes Karṇa(Narakasur) was superior, and sometimes the crowned Arjun was superior. At that time, the snake prince Ashwasen, the son of Takshak who had a great enmity toward Arjun, saw the best opportunity and entered in the quiver of Karṇa in the form of an arrow. When Karṇa could not show more bravery than Arjuna in the war and Arjuna made him very angry with the attack of his arrows, then due to the injury of the arrows, the brave Karṇa thought of attacking with the snake-headed arrow. Therefore, he shot that snake arrow in which Ashwasen was present toward Arjun. As soon as that arrow was released, the sky, in all directions, became blazing. Hundreds of dreadful meteors started falling. As soon as that snake was used on the bow, all the protectors of the world, including Indra, started shouting in an uproar. Even the son of a charioteer did not know that a snake had entered his arrow through the power of yoga. On the other hand, Bhagwan Brahma, seeing Devraj Indra being worried for Arjun, made him ensure that Arjun would win this duel. Seeing that blazing arrow coming with great speed, Lord Krishna, as if playing in the battlefield, immediately pressed his excellent chariot with his foot and sank some part of its wheels into the ground. Along with that, his horses also knelt on the ground. At that time, a great uproar reverberated in the sky from all sides. Suddenly, divine words spoken in praise of Lord Madhusudan started to be heard. When that chariot sank into the ground due to the efforts of Sri Madhusudan, divine flowers started raining on the Lord, and divine lion roars also started appearing. The crown that adorned the head of the wise Arjuna was famous on earth, in space, in heaven and even in Varunaloka. That crown was given to him by Indra. The serpent-headed arrow shot by Karṇa hit Arjuna's head and the crown fall down on the ground due to the chariot being lowered. Thereafter, Ashwasen appeared in his true form in front of them, asking Karṇa(Narakasur) to use him again as an arrow, but Narakasur, within Karṇa, having high moral values, refused his offer. Then Ashwasen, in anger, quickly turned toward Arjun to attack him, and then, on the order of Shree Krishna, he cut down him into pieces with his arrows. After that, Karṇa(Naraksura) wounded both Shree Krishna and Arjun with 10 arrows. Then Arjuna wounded Karṇa with twelve well-shot, sharp arrows called Karṇa(Narakasur) and then pulled a powerful arrow, like a poisonous serpent, up to his ear and released it towards him. That excellent arrow, released with great accuracy, tore apart Karṇa's unique armour and drank his blood as if taking his life; then it sank into the earth. Being heavily wounded by those arrows, Karṇa (Narakasur) aggressively started showering arrows on both Shree Krishna and Arjun, making them wounded. Thereafter, Arjun shot dreadful arrows like Yamdanda at Karṇa. Those feathered arrows pierced his body. Then the excellent, precious and splendid armour of Karṇa, which had been prepared over a long period by the best craftsmen, was broken into many pieces by Pandu's son Arjuna with his arrows in a moment. When Karṇa's armour was cut, Arjuna got angry and injured him again with four very sharp arrows. Being severely injured by the enemy, Karṇa started feeling great pain like a person suffering from fever (tridosha or sannyapaat) related to Vata, Pitta and Kapha. Having been deeply wounded by Arjuna's various types of arrows, which were extremely fast and sharp, Karṇa appeared as beautiful as a mountain with blood oozing out from his body, which, being coloured with metals like red ochre, gushes out red water from its springs. Then again, Arjun pierced his chest with sharp arrows, giving him great pain. After being heavily wounded, his heart was engulfed by fear. Then, due to Brahmin's curse, his chariot wheel got stuck inside the Earth, and at the same time, Parshuram's curse made him forget his Brahmastra's vidya, which Parshursam himself taught him. Thereafter, he jumped on the ground, holding the bow in his hand, but Arjun showered arrows on him even though he was on the ground at that time. Then Karṇa(Narakasur) somehow countered it and cut down two strings of his Gandiva. Thereafter, cursing destiny, he started lifting that wheel and said to Arjun, "Great archer Kuntikumar! Please wait for two moments so that I can remove this stuck wheel from the surface of the earth. O Partha, seeing that by chance my left wheel is stuck to the ground, you should give up your unmanly deceitful behaviour. Pandunandan! You are considered a great warrior and a virtuous person in the world. Do you know the dharma of war? After completing the yagya of the study of Vedanta, you have already taken a bath in it. You know divine weapons. You are full of immortal self-power and are as brave as Kartavirya Arjuna in the battlefield. While I am removing this stuck wheel, you, even though riding the chariot, will keep me standing on the ground, troubled by the attack of arrows. " Then Shree Krishna angrily replied to him,

"Radhanandan! Fortunately, you remember Dharma here! It is often seen that when lowly people are in trouble, they blame destiny and not their evil deeds. Karṇa! When you, Duryodhan, Dushasan and Subalaputra Shakuni called Draupadi, who was menstruating and was wearing only one garment, to the court, did the thought of Dharma arise in your mind at that time? Where did your Dharma go when Shakuni deliberately defeated King Yudhishthira, who did not know about gambling, in the Kaurava Sabha by deceit. Where did your Dharma go when you did not return to the Pandavas' kingdom even after the thirteenth year of their exile had passed? Where did your Dharma go when King Duryodhana, taking your advice, fed Bhimasen food laced with poison and got him bitten by snakes?Where did your Dharma go when you tried to burn the sons of Kunti who were sleeping in Lakhsha Bhavan in Varanavatnagar? Where did your Dharma go when you ridiculed Draupadi, who was menstruating and under the control of Dushasan in the presence of everyone? Where did your Dharma go when you were closely watching the innocent Draupadi being tortured by the vile Kauravas? Where did your Dharma go when, in the war, along with many of you great warriors, you surrounded the child Abhimanyu from all sides and killed him? If this was not Dharma on those occasions, then what is the use of pleasing the palate by invoking Dharma here, even today? O Sut! No matter how many acts of Dharma you perform here, you will not be able to be freed from your sins while you are alive. "

 At that time, when Lord Krishna said this, Karṇa bowed his head in shame and was unable to give any answer. Then, being endowed with great speed and valour, he took up his bow, his lips flapping in anger and began to fight with Arjuna. Then Arjun summoned Brahmastra and released it at Karṇa (Narakasur). And then, due to Parshuram's Curse, he wasn't able to counter it, and thus, it cut off Karṇa's (Narakasur) head, making the world free from the terrors of Karṇa and Narakasur once and for all. The moment when both Karṇa and Narakasur died, devatas started raining flowers on Arjun and Shree Krishna, congratulating them for their victory. On listening about Karṇa's death, King Yudhisthir become very happy and welcomes both Shree Krishna and Arjun gladly. On the other hand, Duryodhan got broken completely and withdrew his army from the Battlefield. Therefore, it concludes as a victory for Pandavs.

THE END OF THE WAR

After the death of Karṇa, Duryodhana, in consultation with Ashwatthama, appointed King Shalya as the new commander-in-chief of the Kuru army. Thereafter, under Shalya's leadership, the war of the eighteenth day began. As the battle commenced, Shalya displayed extraordinary valour, piercing through the ranks of the Pandava warriors and wounding many of them badly. Seeing this, Shree Krishna advised Yudhishthira to personally confront and kill Shalya. Following his advice, Yudhishthira advanced toward Shalya, and a fierce duel began between them, so intense that it became difficult to predict who would emerge victorious. Meanwhile, Arjuna and Bhimasena unleashed devastation on the rest of the Kuru army, killing everything that stood in their way. Arjuna finally destroyed the entire Trigarta army and beheaded Susharma along with his brothers and son, thus fulfilling his vow. Bhimasena killed eleven more sons of Dhritarashtra along with Sudarshana, bringing the total to ninety-nine slain sons of Dhritarashtra—leaving only Duryodhana alive. After destroying the Trigarta forces, Arjuna went on to defeat Ashwatthama, Kripacharya, and Kritavarma, forcing all three to flee the battlefield. Meanwhile, in the fierce duel between Shalya and Yudhishthira, Yudhishthira finally killed Shalya with a spear, leaving the Kuru army leaderless and directionless. On another front, Sahadeva killed Shakuni along with his son Uluka, taking revenge for the deceitful game of dice. Witnessing the slaughter of his allies, the Mleccha king Shalva mounted his elephant and began terrorizing the Pandava army. Then, Drishtadyumna first killed the Mleccha king's elephant, and as the elephant collapsed to the ground, Satyaki cut off the king's head. Thereafter, Duryodhana, seeing that his entire army had been destroyed along with all the great warriors and generals, and having been severely wounded himself, fled the battlefield and hid in a pond to save his life. However, the Pandavas later found him, and Bhimasena defeated him by striking his thigh with his mace, thus fulfilling the vow he had taken in the Kaurava sabha and bringing an end to the dark era of the Kauravas. After Duryodhana's defeat, Ashwatthama, accompanied by Kripacharya and Kritavarma, came to see him. Seeing Duryodhana in such a pitiful condition, Ashwatthama was filled with rage and took a vow to annihilate the Pandava army. That night, in the absence of Shree Krishna, the Pandavas, and Satyaki, Ashwatthama infiltrated their camp with Kripacharya and Kritavarma and massacred everyone present. When the Pandavas learned of this treachery, they were furious and confronted Ashwatthama. In response, Ashwatthama launched the Brahmastra at them, and Arjuna countered with his own Brahmastra. Sage Ved Vyasa intervened and ordered both warriors to withdraw their celestial weapons. Arjuna, being knowledgeable, successfully withdrew his weapon, but Ashwatthama, unable to do so, redirected his Brahmastra toward the womb of Uttara, thereby attempting to destroy the last hope of the Pandavas' lineage. In response, Shree Krishna took away Ashwatthama's divine gem and cursed him to wander the Earth in misery until the end of Kaliyuga. He also vowed to revive Abhimanyu's unborn son, and later fulfilled this promise by bringing the dead child back to life. Thereafter, Yudhishthira was crowned as the king of Bharatvarsha, and after a long and difficult struggle, he established the righteous rule of Dharma across the land.

CONCLUSION

Karṇa wasn't as great as modern TV shows and writers portray him. He was a man filled with hatred and driven by a false ego as vast as the Himalayan mountains. It was Karṇa who planted the seeds of malice in Duryodhana's mind, suggesting sinister plans to kill the Pandavas—from poisoning Bhīmasena to plotting their death in the Lakshagraha at Varnavrat. His enmity towards the Pandavas ran so deep that he didn't hesitate to insult Sati Draupadi in a public assembly. In fact, it was Karṇa who ordered Duśśāsana to disrobe Draupadi, the Kulvadhu of the illustrious Kuru dynasty, merely to gratify his hatred and twisted sense of pride. Even during the Pandavas' exile, he once again urged Duryodhana to capture and kill the Pandavas and seize Draupadi, a plan that Sage Vyasa himself thwarted. Karṇa was not the unparalleled warrior he is often claimed to be—unlike Bhīṣma or Droṇacharya. He was repeatedly defeated by Arjuna, Bhīmasena, Satyaki, the Gandharvas, and even Draupadi. His so-called successes, including the Digvijaya Yatra and his fierce battles during the Kurukshetra war, were only possible because of Narakasura's possession of his body. Without that influence, Arjuna would likely have killed him even earlier, during the Virata War. Ultimately, Karṇa was neither noble in character nor unmatched in battle. He was a man consumed by bitterness and ego, who allied with Duryodhana solely out of hatred for Arjuna. As Mahatma Shree Krishna rightfully said in the Udyoga Parva, Karṇa's role in Duryodhana's life was not of a wise counselor or virtuous ally, but of a destructive force rooted in enmity and arrogance

सुयोधनो मन्युमयो महाद्रुमःस्कन्धःकर्णःशकुनिस्तस्य
शाखाः। दुःशासनःपुष्पफले समृद्धे मूलं राजा
धृतराष्ट्रोऽमनीषी

Duryodhan is like a huge tree full of anger, Karṇa is the trunk of that tree, Shakuni is the branch and Dushasan is the rich fruit and flower. Ignorant king Dhritarashtra is its root.

(Udyoga Parva,Sanjayayan Parv,chap 29 ,shlok 52)

Karna is the mastermind behind the all evil act of Duryodhan.

ABOUT THE AUTHOR

Akshat Dubey, a revered author, has been interested in Indian History since childhood. He has always been a person who believes in seeing the Indian Tradition through the lens of the Scriptures. Tasmat Shastram Pramanam Te, Karya Karyau Vivasthitau. This means that the scriptures are only proof.

He is currently pursuing his B.A. L.LB. in Prayagraj, wishes to further work in the direction of self-development through the paths of Vaidik Traditions.